CONTEMPORARY'S

Put English To Work

LEVEL 2

INTERACTION AND COMPETENCIES
FOR JOB SUCCESS

JANET PODNECKY

SERIES ADVISOR
CAROLE ETCHELLS CROSS

CB

CONTEMPORARY BOOKS

a division of NTC/CONTEMPORARY PUBLISHING GROUP
Lincolnwood, Illinois USA

Publisher: Steve VanThournout
Editorial Director: Cindy Krejcsi
Executive Editor: Mary Jane Maples
Editor: Michael O'Neill
Director, World Languages Publishing: Keith Fry
Art Director: Ophelia M. Chambliss
Cover and Interior Design: Michael Kelly
Fine Art Illustrations: Adam Young
Line Art Illustrations: David Will
Production Manager: Margo Goia

Acknowledgments begin on page vi, which is to be considered
an extension of this copyright page.

ISBN: 0-8092-3358-4

Published by Contemporary Books,
a division of NTC/Contemporary Publishing Group, Inc.,
4255 West Touhy Avenue,
Lincolnwood (Chicago), Illinois 60712-1975 U.S.A.

0 1 2 3 4 5 6 7 8 9   VH   15 14 13 12 11 10 9 8 7 6 5 4

Contents

Put English to Work is a seven-level interactive workplace-literacy course for students of English as a second or foreign language. The series spans the entire range of levels usually taught in ESL/EFL programs—from the beginning-literacy level to the high-advanced level. A communicative, competency-based program, *Put English to Work* features an integrated syllabus focusing on workplace competencies, general English-language skills, communicative functions, form, and culture. The content of each text has been carefully planned to meet the curricular, instructional, and level requirements of California's state standards for adult ESL programs.

The format of *Put English to Work* is designed for maximum flexibility and ease of use. Teachers in a variety of programs—from vocational ESL and workplace ESL programs to general ESL programs with a school-to-work focus—will find this series ideal for their instructional needs. In addition, teachers who work with multilevel classes will find these texts useful with almost any combination of levels because of the cross-level coverage of a number of the most important workplace topics. *Put English to Work* consists of the following components:

- Seven student books, from Literacy Level to Level 6
- Seven teacher's guides, one for each level
- Seven audiocassettes, one for each level

Each student book contains a Picture Dictionary at the back—an additional resource offering teachers a variety of strategies for vocabulary building. The teacher's guides contain extension activities, sample lesson plans, and suggestions on adaptation of the materials to a number of different teaching styles and programs, from integration of grammar to using the materials in multilevel settings. The teacher's guides also contain the tapescripts for the audiocassettes, which are available separately.

The philosophy behind *Put English to Work*—spelled out in greater detail in the teacher's guides—is interactive and competency-based. The series places a strong emphasis on developing the four language skills—listening, speaking, reading, and writing—in conjunction with critical thinking, problem solving, and computation skills. An important feature is the incorporation of the SCANS competencies, developed by the Secretary's Commission on Achieving Necessary Skills in a project sponsored by the Department of Labor. In addition, the series focuses on a great number of the competencies within the Comprehensive Adult Student Assessment System (CASAS).

Skills are taught within an integrated framework that emphasizes meaningful and purposeful use of language in realistic contexts to develop communicative competence. Target language, structures, and functions are presented in contexts that are relevant to students' lives. Students need to learn strategies and skills to function in real-life situations—in particular, those related to job search and the workplace. Other situations and life-skill areas are covered as well, notably health, family, and community resources.

The cultural focus of *Put English to Work* not only presents aspects of U.S. culture that many students need to come to grips with, but also allows for a free exchange of ideas about values and situations that people from different cultures naturally view differently. In the process, students learn about the culture that informs the U.S. workplace while understanding that their own cultural perspectives are intrinsically valuable.

Level 2 of *Put English to Work* is geared toward learners at the high-beginning level. Level 2 presumes a limited ability to read and write in English. In addition, students at this level have limited listening and speaking skills. A certain amount of the skills of Level 1 are reviewed in Level 2, and teachers with classes of mixed beginning-level students may wish to use Level 2 in conjunction with the Level 1 text. Suggestions for use of the two levels are provided in the teacher's guides for these levels.

Level 2 focuses on the development of beginning-level language skills, document literacy, and understanding of workplace vocabulary and culture through the presentation of realistic workplace contexts. Clarification skills are presented and practiced throughout the level. Vocabulary is represented by glosses and illustrations, including the opening illustration of each unit, the illustrations in the vocabulary section of each unit, and the Picture Dictionary at the end of the book.

The SCANS competencies targeted in Level 2 are the following:

Allocating material resources
Allocating human resources
Acquiring and evaluating information
Interpreting and communicating information
Organizing and maintaining information
Teaching others
Participating as a member of a team
Working with people of culturally diverse backgrounds
Understanding systems

Acknowledgments

The authors and publisher of *Put English to Work* would like to thank the consultants, reviewers, and fieldtesters who helped to make this series possible, including Gretchen Bitterlin, San Diego Community College, San Diego, CA; Ann de Cruz, Elgin Community College, Elgin, IL; Greta Grossman, New York Association for New Americans, New York, NY; Bet Messmer, Educational Options, Santa Clara, CA; Michael Roddy, Salinas Adult School, Salinas, CA; Federico Salas, North Harris Montgomery County Community College, Houston, TX; Terry Shearer, Houston Community College, Houston, TX. Special thanks to Mark Boone.

Unit 1
JOB SERVICES

Look at the picture. Point to these signs:

Employment and Training Office   Workshops
Job Openings   Job Hotline

Where are they? What are they doing? What are they talking about?

1 Listen and Think

Listen and circle the correct answers.

1. Who is looking for a job?	A	B	Ⓒ
2. What job are they talking about?	a. mechanic	b. janitor	c. nurse's aide
3. When is the workshop?	a. Tues. 7:00	b. Mon. 6:00	c. Fri. 4:00
4. What is the phone number for the hotline?	a. 622-5454	b. 622-5544	c. 622-7544

2 Talk to a Partner

Step 1. Practice the conversation with a partner.

A: I'm looking for a job.
B: What work experience do you have?
A: Well, I was a **carpenter** in **Haiti**.
B: When were you a **carpenter**?
A: From **1994 to 1996**.

Step 2. Change partners. Practice the conversation again. Use other jobs.

3 Read and Think

Step 1. Look at the picture on the right.
This is Raymond Sedar.

Step 2. Read the time line below.
When did Raymond Sedar arrive
in the U.S. from Haiti?

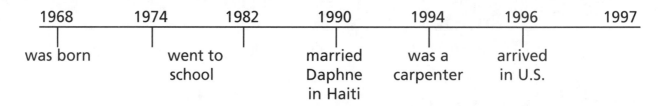

1968	1974	1982	1990	1994	1996	1997
was born	went to school		married Daphne in Haiti	was a carpenter	arrived in U.S.	

Step 3. Read the text.

Raymond Sedar was born in Haiti in 1968. He was a student from 1974 to 1982. In 1990 he married Daphne Carnes. Raymond was a carpenter for two years in Haiti. He worked from 1994 to 1996. Then in 1996 Raymond and his family came to the U.S.

Now Raymond is at the Employment and Training Office. He wants some help looking for a job.

Step 4. Look at the vocabulary on page 3. There are many different kinds of jobs.

Vocabulary

Jobs and Activities

an assembler

He puts the parts together.

a machine operator

She operates the machine to make the parts.

a machinist

He fixes the machines in the factory.

a florist

She arranges and sells flowers.

a baker

She bakes bread and cakes.

a butcher

He cuts meat.

a hairstylist

She cuts men's and women's hair.

a mechanic

He fixes cars.

a welder

He does welding.

Word Match

A. Write the jobs in the right workplaces.

TOP STAR RESTAURANT

_____

_____

_____

FURNITURE FACTORY

_____

_____

_____

**GREEN THUMB
FLOWER SHOP**

_____

**PERFECT TOUCH HAIR STYLING
FOR MEN AND WOMEN**

_____

_____

B. Match the activities with the jobs.

1. bake bread

2. cut meat

3. operate a machine

4. put parts together

5. arrange and sell flowers

6. fix and adjust machines

7. cut and style hair

a. assembler

b. florist

c. machinist

d. baker

e. butcher

f. hairstylist

g. machine operator

4 Put It in Writing

Answer these questions.

1. What's your name? _____

2. What's your Social Security Number? _____

3. What work experience do you have? _____

4. When were you a _____ ? _____

5. Where did you work? _____

6. Why did you leave your job? _____

5 Listen and Speak

Step 1. Listen to the conversation.

Counselor: What kind of a job are you looking for?
        A: I'm not sure. I was a **math teacher**
             before.
Counselor: Where was that?
        A: In **Mexico**.
Counselor: How long were you a **teacher**?
        A: For **five years**.
Counselor: Why did you leave your job?
        A: Because **I came to the U.S.**
Counselor: Do you speak **Spanish**?
        A: Yes, I do.
Counselor: There's a job opening for a **bilingual teacher's aide**.
        A: That sounds interesting.

Step 2. Practice the conversation with a partner.

Step 3. Change partners. Practice again using your own past jobs.

6 Read and Write

Step 1. Read the information on the form.

Employment & Training Services

Name _Sara Nelson_   **SSN** _644-03-2773_

Address _3115 Commonwealth Avenue, Apt. 14_   **Tel.** _273-0781_

Boston, MA 02125

Work Experience

	Job Title	Location	Dates	Reason for Leaving
1.	Bookkeeper	Southwest Bank	4/95-9/96	Moved
		Los Angeles, CA		
2.	Bank Teller	Southwest Bank	4/93-4/95	Offered better job
		Los Angeles, CA		

Other Skills and Abilities

I can type and use a computer. I can speak Spanish.

Signature _Sara Nelson_   **Date** _5/22/97_

Step 2. Write the answers to the questions.

1. What's Sara's Social Security Number? _644-03-2773_

2. How many jobs did she have? _____

3. What jobs did she have? _____

4. Where did she work? _____

5. When did she work as a bank teller? _____

6. Why did she leave her last job? _____

Step 3. With a partner, compare your answers.

Form and Function

1 I'm not a math teacher anymore.

not						
I	**am not**	a carpenter.	**I'm not**	a carpenter.		
You	**are not**	a carpenter.	**You're not**	a carpenter.	**You aren't**	a carpenter.
He	**is not**	a carpenter.	**He's not**	a carpenter.	**He isn't**	a carpenter.
She	**is not**	a carpenter.	**She's not**	a carpenter.	**She isn't**	a carpenter.
It	**is not**	a table.	**It's not**	a table.	**It isn't**	a table.
We	**are not**	carpenters.	**We're not**	carpenters.	**We aren't**	carpenters.
They	**are not**	carpenters.	**They're not**	carpenters.	**They aren't**	carpenters.

not . . . anymore

Joan worked at the factory five years ago.
She doesn't work at the factory now.

She	**doesn't**	work at the factory **anymore**.
	does **not**	

no more

They had envelopes yesterday.
They don't have envelopes today.

They have **no more** envelopes.

Examples

Does he live there?

No, he does**n't**.

Do you have an envelope?

No, I do**n't**. I have **no more** envelopes in my desk.

Are you still working in the hospital?

No, I **don't** work there **anymore**. Now I work at the clinic.

Practice 1

A. Listen. Circle the word(s) you hear.

1. (not) no more no longer

2. not no more no longer

3. not no more no longer

4. not no more no longer

5. not no more no longer

6. not no more no longer

B. Circle the correct words.

1. Do you have any coffee?   No, we have (**no more** **not anymore**) coffee.

2. Is Mark still studying at the university? No, he's not there (**no more**   **anymore**).

3. Can I borrow some money?   Sorry, I have (**no more**   **not anymore**) money.

4. Do you still go to the farmer's market?   No, we don't go there (**no more**   **anymore**).

5. Is your sister still visiting?   No, she's not here (**no more**   **anymore**).

2 A: Do you speak Spanish? B: Yes, I do.

I You We They	speak	I You We They	do not (don't)	Do	I you we they	speak?
He She It	speaks	He She It	does not (doesn't)	Does	he she it	speak?

Examples

Where do they **live**?   They **live** in Boston.
What does she **assemble**?   She **assembles** computers.
Do you **like** to read?   No, I **don't**.
When does the train **arrive**?   It **arrives** at 10:00.

Practice 2

A. Listen. Circle the word you hear.

1. help   (helps)   4. count   counts

2. answer   answers   5. wash   washes

3. fix   fixes   6. leave   leaves

B. Fill in the correct form of the verbs in the sentences.

1. We _____*finish*_____ (finish) class at 8:00.

2. Anton _____ (start) work at 2:00.

3. On Saturday I _____ (clean) the kitchen.

4. _____ they _____ (work) in a factory?

5. When _____ she _____ (watch) TV?

6. We _____ n't _____ (eat) in restaurants often.

7. You _____ n't _____ (like) to cook.

8. _____ he _____ (play) on the soccer team?

C. Work with a partner. Ask questions with *do/does*.
Student A: Look at this page. Student B: Look at page 10. Ask your partner about the people below. Fill in the missing information.

Example: A: Where does Masha live? B: She lives in Boston.

	Where? (live)	Where? (work)	When? (study)	What languages? (speak)
Masha	lives in Boston	works in a clinic		speaks Russian and English
Allan	lives in Malden		doesn't study	
Kim and Tung		don't work		speak Chinese and English
(you)				

**Work with a partner. Student B: Look at this page. Student A: Look at page 9.
Ask your partner about the people below. Fill in the missing information.**

Example: A: Where does Masha live? B: She lives in Boston.

	Where? (live)	Where? (work)	When? (study)	What languages? (speak)
Masha	lives in Boston		studies at night	
Allan		works in a factory		speaks Spanish and English
Kim and Tung	live in Brookline		study in the morning	
(you)				

With your partner, compare your answers.

D. Now write sentences with the information in the chart.

1. Masha _lives in Boston._ _____

_____

_____

2. Allan _____

_____

_____

3. Kim and Tung _____

_____

_____

4. My partner (_____) _____

_____

_____

Putting It to Work

Step 1. Listen and fill in the missing information from the telephone message.

MEMO

For _Mr. Martin_ _____ **Date** _6/30_ _____

Time _____ AM/PM

While you were out . . .

_____ called. Phone # _____

/ / called   / / returned your call   / / will call back
/ / please call   / / left a message   / / _____

Message: _____

_____

_____

Taken by:

Step 2. With a partner, compare your answers.

Step 3. Role-play. Practice giving the message orally to the person.

2 Pair Work

Step 1. Make a time line of important events in your life.

now

——|————

Step 2. Tell your partner about your life.

Step 3. Listen as your partner talks about his or her life. Mark the dates and events on the time line below.

now

——|————

Step 4. Now compare your time lines.

3 Group/Class Work

Step 1. In a group, read about the people below.

Step 2. Discuss this question: Which jobs are right for them? Explain your opinion to the group.

Hung-Ju was a machinist in Korea for eight years. He worked in a car factory. He can operate and fix many machines.

Job A security guard in a car factory	Job B machine operator in a computer factory	Job C taxi driver

Maria was a science teacher for five years. She is good with emergencies and first aid. She likes to work with people.

Job D nurse's aide in a hospital	Job E clerk in a shoe store	Job F kitchen helper in a restaurant

Step 3. Make a group list of your ideas.

Step 4. Tell the class.

4 Culture Work

What jobs do people have? Are jobs the same or different in the U.S. and in your native country? Make two lists and compare them. Tell the class.

1. Jobs in the U.S.   2. Jobs in my native country

Job Titles

painter	receptionist	fisherman	cook
clerk	secretary	farmer	dishwasher
janitor	computer programmer	soldier	waiter
bus driver	housekeeper	police officer	nurse
taxi driver	childcare worker	firefighter	nurse's aide
teacher	paramedic	cashier	mechanic
welder	assembler	salesperson	
machinist	machine operator	florist	

Unit 2
HELP WANTED

Openers

Look at the picture and the ad below. Point to these things and words:

newspaper   ads   experience

benefits   hours   pay

Where is she? What is she doing? What is she talking about?

1 Listen and Think

Listen and circle the correct information on the ad.

> **NURSE'S AIDE/LAB WORKER**
>
> position available
> Experience necessary / No experience necessary
> Full-Time / Part-Time
> Pay: $5.25 / $6.55 per hour
> Benefits / No Benefits
> Hours: Morning / Evening Shift
> Call Pat Garvin: 432-8800

2 Talk to a Partner

Step 1. Practice the conversation with a partner.

A: I'm calling about the ad for **a bus driver**.
B: OK, we still have an opening for **a bus driver**.
Can you **drive a bus**?
A: Yes, I can.
B: Come in and fill out an application.
A: OK. Thank you.

Bus Driver Wanted,
Morning and afternoons.
Call 247–5757

Experienced Wait Staff to
serve breakfast and lunch.
Call 422–4348

Legal Secretary,
Must type and answer phones.
733–7755

Hair Stylist, Sylvia's
Hair Salon, Need experienced
stylist to cut & style women's hair.
775–8282

Step 2. Change partners. Practice the conversation again. Use the other ads.

3 Read and Think

Step 1. Look at the picture. Elenora is looking through the help wanted ads.

Step 2. Read the text.

Elenora is looking for a new job.
She looks for ads in the newspaper, at
the employment agency, and at other
places around town. Elenora reads each
ad carefully. She checks the skills needed,
the hours, the pay, and how to apply.
There are openings for lab assistants at
the clinic and at the hospital. Tomorrow
she's going to go and fill out some
applications. She hopes to get a new
job soon.

Vocabulary

Jobs and Skills

a pharmacist

He prepares medicines.

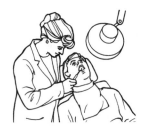

a dentist

She checks teeth.

a dental assistant

He helps clean teeth.

a switchboard operator

He answers phones at a large company.

a typist

She types letters and papers.

a file clerk

She organizes papers.

a photographer

He takes pictures.

a travel agent

She arranges trips and vacations.

Word Match

A. Match the jobs with the workplaces.

1. **Westwood Dental Clinic**

2. **Get Away Travel Agency**
   Let us plan your vacation!

3. **Central Photo Studio**
   When a picture is worth more . . .

4. *Main Street Pharmacy*
   Prescription medicines and more

a. pharmacist

b. photographer

c. dental assistant

d. travel agent

B. Circle the job that does the work.

1. types reports and letters   **a.** file clerk   **b.** typist   **c.** doctor

2. takes care of teeth   **a.** photographer   **b.** cook   **c.** dentist

3. helps arrange a trip   **a.** travel agent   **b.** secretary   **c.** bus driver

4. gets medicine for you   **a.** machinist   **b.** pharmacist   **c.** file clerk

5. answers and directs phone calls in a large company   **a.** switchboard operator   **b.** manager   **c.** nurse

6. organizes papers and files   **a.** baker   **b.** file clerk   **c.** cashier

4 Put It in Writing

Answer these questions.

1. What can Stella do? _____

2. What job does she want? _____

3. What can Tran do? _____

4. What job does he want? _____

5. What can you do? _____

6. What job do you want? _____

5 Listen and Speak

Step 1. Listen to the conversation.

> A: Do you have any job openings for **bakers**?
> B: Yes, we do. But you need experience.
> A: I worked as **a baker** for **six months**.
> B: Can you work **mornings**?
> A: Yes. What are the hours?
> B: **3:00 A.M. to 11 A.M. five days a week.**
> A: That's OK. How much is the pay?
> B: **$6.55** per hour.

HELP WANTED	HELP WANTED
BAKERS needed, mornings 3 a.m.–11 a.m. Full-time $6.55 an hour	**DENTAL ASSISTANT** part-time, afternoons 12–5, 3 days/wk. $5.75 an hour

Step 2. Practice the conversation with a partner.

Step 3. Change partners. Practice again using the other ad.

6 Read and Write

Step 1. Read the information in the ads.

Hillside Nursing Home has openings for the following positions: Nurse-FT day shift Nurse's Aide-PT day and evening hours 588-8047

Office helper needed to work in busy legal firm. Must do word processing. M, T, Th, 12–5 P.M. Call Paula 623-4744.

Step 2. Write the answers to the questions.

1. Which job is full-time? _The nursing job._

2. Which job is in the afternoon? _____

3. What does the office helper do? _____

4. When does the nurse work? _____

5. What days does the office helper work? _____

6. What's the phone number for the nursing home? _____

Step 3. With a partner, compare your answers.

1 I'm calling about the ad.

I'm		I'm not		Am I	
You're		You aren't		Are you	
He's		He isn't		Is he	
She's	**working.**	She isn't	**working.**	Is she	**working?**
We're		We aren't		Are we	
They're		They aren't		Are they	

Examples

My sister **is working** at the bank right now.
Is she **going** to school, too?   No, she **isn't going** to school this term.
What are you **studying**?   **I'm studying** English.

Practice 1

A. Listen. Circle the word you hear.

1. (calling)   call   **4.** visiting   visit

2. walking   walk   **5.** fixing   fixes

3. looking   looks   **6.** taking   take

B. Fill in the missing words.

1. Where are you going?

   I *'m going* _____ to the library.

2. Who's working in Room 201?

   Joe and Ray _____ in Room 201.

3. Is Peter writing a letter?

   No, he _____ a letter.

   He _____ a book.

4. Are they taking pictures now?

   No, they _____ pictures.

   They _____ TV.

5. What are you doing?

   I _____.

2   I worked as a baker before.

Every day		Yesterday	
I call my friend after work.		I call**ed** her at 8:00.	
(call)	call**ed**	(be)	**was/were**
(work)	work**ed**	(do)	**did**
(ask)	ask**ed**	(have)	**had**
(visit)	visit**ed**	(go)	**went**
(arrive)	arriv**ed**	(see)	**saw**
(stop)	stopp**ed**	(take)	**took**
(carry)	carr**ied**	(give)	**gave**

Examples

I **was** a teacher in my country.

When did you **start** this job?

Did she **work** yesterday?

Did Sally **go** to the beach?

I **worked** in a school.

I **started** last week.

No, she **didn't work** yesterday.

No, she **didn't go** to the beach. She **went** to the movies instead.

Practice 2

A. Listen. Circle the word you hear.

1. help   (helped)   4. count   counted   7. see   saw

2. answer   answered   5. wash   washed   8. do   did

3. fix   fixed   6. move   moved   9. give   gave

B. Fill in the correct form of the verbs in the sentences.

1. We _____watched_____ (watch) a soccer match last weekend.

2. The team _____ (play) well.

3. The score _____ (be) 2–1.

4. I _____ (take) some pictures of the game.

5. We _____ (have) a good time.

6. Mark _____ (see) an ad in the paper for a job.

7. Later Mark _____ (go) and _____ (fill) out an application.

C. Work with a partner. Ask and answer questions. Student A: Look at this page. Student B: Look at page 22. Ask about the people below. Circle the answers.

Example: A: Did Mitch go to New York or California? B: He went to New York.

	(go)?	(see)?	(take)?
Mitch	(New York) California	his sister his brother	a bus a train
Amy	the park the store	her friend her cousin	a taxi a walk
Victor and Linda	Washington Chicago	their friends their children	an airplane a boat

Now tell your partner about these people.

Alice went to Florida and saw her parents. She took an airplane.

Kevin went to Canada. He saw his uncle. He took a train.

Julia and Daniel went to Chicago. They saw their friends. They took a bus.

Work with a partner. Ask and answer questions. Student B: Look at this page. Student A: Look at page 21. Answer your partner's questions about the people below.

Mitch went to New York.
He saw his brother.
He took a train.

Amy went to the park.
She saw her friend. She took
a taxi.

Victor and Linda went to
Chicago. They saw their
children. They took an
airplane.

Now ask questions about the people in the chart below. Circle the answers.

Example: B: Did Alice go to Virginia or Florida? A: She went to Florida.

	(go)?	(see)?	(take)?
Alice	Virginia Florida	her cousins her parents	an airplane a bus
Kevin	Canada Mexico	his uncle his brother	a train an airplane
Julia and Daniel	Washington Chicago	their children their friends	a boat a bus

With your partner, compare your answers.

D. Choose two people from the chart and write three sentences about each of them. Use the information from the chart.

1. _____

   _____

   _____

2. _____

   _____

   _____

Putting It to Work

1 Pair Work

Step 1. Listen and fill in the missing information on the want ads.

Job Notice
_____
$ _____ /hr.
_____ time
Good benefits
Call _____

Help Wanted
_____
$ _____ /hr.
_____ days/wk.
Hours: _____
Call _____

Step 2. With a partner, compare your answers. Role-play a phone conversation. Call and ask about these job openings.

2 Pair Work

Step 1. With a partner, read the ads below.

COOKS
Needed full time, morning and evening shifts.

HAIRDRESSER
Experienced in styling, cutting, and perms. Carla's Beauty Salon. 766-4331.

WANTED
Seamstress for sewing, mending, and alterations. Westside Cleaners, 822 Bradley St.

TYPIST
Needed for busy insurance office. Apply in person: Corcoran Insurance Co., 331 Main St.

BAKER
Immediate need for baker. Early morning shift. Sun-Up Bakery. Call 654-3434.

AUTO MECHANIC
Full-time. Need own tools. Stan's Garage. 41 Oak St.

Step 2. Think about your friends and acquaintances. Who are the right people for these jobs? Talk about the people in your class and the people you know. Try to think of people for at least three jobs.

Example:

A: My brother is looking for a job.
B: What does he do?
A: He takes pictures. He's a photographer.
B: Oh, well, Wilson Photo Shop needs a photographer.
A: Oh, I'll tell him.

Step 3. With a partner, role-play a conversation about one of the people for one of the jobs above. Tell your friend, classmate, or acquaintance about the job.

3 Group/Class Work

Step 1. Look at the want ads. With a group, think of the skills needed for each job and fill them in below.

| Help Wanted: **Switchboard Operator** ———— ———— Full-time, good benefits. Call Mark: 442-9885 | Quality Portraits Inc. **Photographer needed.** ———— ———— Must work weekends. Pay according to experience. 766-6440 | Immediate Openings: **File Clerk** ———— ———— Part-time, $4.75/hr. Payson Law Office, 343-7700 | Milton Travel Agency Needs **Travel Agent** ———— ———— Will train. Part-time. Pay according to experience, plus commissions. 565-5522. |

Do you like any of these jobs? Why or why not?

_____

_____

Step 2. Think of some questions about these jobs. Write your questions on the lines below.

_____

_____

Step 3. Discuss your questions about the jobs with your group. Then tell the class.

4 Culture Work

What types of jobs are there in your country? What types of jobs are there in the United States? Are they the same or different? Talk about it with your class.

	Jobs in my country	Jobs I see in the United States
Hours		
Pay		
Benefits		
Full/Part-time		
Advantages		
Disadvantages		

Unit 3
APPOINTMENTS AND INTERVIEWS

Openers

Look at the picture. Point to these things and people:

receptionist
file cabinet

application
brochure

clipboard

Where are they? What are they doing? What are they talking about?

1 Listen and Think

Listen to the conversations. Then circle the correct answers.

1. Who did Elenora talk to yesterday?   **a.** the receptionist   **b.** Pat Garvin

2. What job is she applying for?   **a.** a dental assistant   **b.** a lab worker

3. What does she need to fill out?   **a.** an application   **b.** a clipboard

4. Can Elenora come on Friday at 2:00?   **a.** yes   **b.** no

5. When can she come?   **a.** 10:30   **b.** 1:30

2 Talk to a Partner

Step 1. Practice the conversations with a partner.

A: Excuse me. Do you have any openings for a **nurse's aide**?
B: Yes, we do. Would you like to fill out an application?
A: Yes, please.

B: Can you come in for an interview on **Friday** at **11:00**?
A: Oh, can I come **in the afternoon**?
B: Is **3:00** OK?
A: That will be fine. Thank you.

Monday 10:00 p.m. 11:00 a.m.
Tuesday Sunday
WEDNESDAY THURSDAY Saturday
9:00 a.m.
Friday 3:30 p.m. 5:30 p.m.
2:00 p.m. *in the morning, later, earlier, in the afternoon*

Step 2. Change partners. Practice the conversations again. Use other jobs, days, and times.

3 Read and Think

Step 1. Look at the picture. Elenora is preparing for an interview.

Step 2. Read the text.

Elenora's interview is tomorrow. Today she's preparing for the interview. She's making a list of possible questions: What work experience do you have? Do you have experience in a hospital or clinic? Why do you want this job?

Elenora is also reading the brochure about the clinic. It will help her learn about the job. She is going to ask some questions at the interview about the pay, the hours, benefits, and training.

Step 3. Look at the vocabulary on page 27. Then re

Vocabulary

Job Skills

He **attaches** the papers.

She **collects** the glasses from the tables.

The cook **weighs** the food.

He **measures** the window.

She **records** the numbers.

He **examines** the pants.

Job Terms

salary money paid for work
skills what a worker can do
references people who know you

overtime more than 40 hours of work/week
supervisor the person in charge
benefits extra things you get for working

Word Match

A. Write the skills in the sentences.

1. I'm a nurse's aide. I _____*collect*_____ the breakfast trays from the rooms.

   a. measure

2. Sometimes I _____ the patients. This baby girl is 12 pounds.

   b. record

3. After that I _____ her. She is 24 inches long.

   c. collect

4. I _____ the information on a chart for the patient.

   d. attach

5. I hold the baby. The nurse will come and

   _____ the baby's eyes and ears.

   e. examine

6. I take all the papers and _____ them. Then I put them in the file cabinet.

   f. weigh

B. Draw a line from the information to the word.

salary

overtime

skills

> **Line/prep cook** needed. Must have experience broiling and grilling. 40 hours / week. Additional hours and pay on holidays. Pay $7.25 to start. Also insurance, vacation, sick time. Apply in person to Tony, head chef at Parkview Restaurant. Bring names of three past employers.

references

supervisor

benefits

4 Put It in Writing

Answer these questions.

1. What skills do you have? _____

2. What salary do you want? _____

3. Are you working now? _____

4. Who is your supervisor? _____

5. What benefits do you want? _____

6. Who can you use as a reference for your work? _____

5 Listen and Speak

Step 1. Listen to the conversation.

> A: Do you have any experience as a nurse?
> B: Well, yes. I was a **nursing student in Costa Rica.**
>   **I studied for one year,** and then I came to the U.S.
> A: Why do you want to work here?
> B: I like to **help people**. I think I can learn a lot.
> A: Can you start to work on **August 15th**?
> B: Can I begin on the **22nd**?
> A: That will be all right.

Step 2. Practice the conversation with a partner.

Step 3. Change partners. Practice again. Use your own past experience and other dates.

6 Read and Write

Step 1.   Read the information on the form.

Application for Employment

Personal Data

Name _Elenora Rivas_

Work Experience

Job Title	**Location**	**Length of Time**
1. _Childcare worker_	_1, 2, 3 Day School_	_1 year_
2. _Waitress_	_Pete's Steakhouse_	_8 months_

Check the skills you have

__✓__ typing   ____ shorthand   ____ word processing

____ computer   ____ other _____

References (Not Relatives)

Name	**Address**	**Phone**	**Business**
1. _Sara Nelson_	_1, 2, 3 Day School, 25 Park Drive_	_623-4433_	_Teacher_
2. _Hector Cortes_	_Pete's Steakhouse, 880 Main St._	_721-9698_	_Manager_

Step 2.   Write the answers to the questions.

1. Who is applying for a job? _Elenora Rivas is._

2. How many jobs did she have? _____

3. Who was her supervisor at Pete's Steakhouse? _____

4. What office skills does she have? _____

5. How long did she work at the day-care center? _____

6. Who is Sara Nelson? Why do you think she listed her as a reference? _____

_____

Step 3.   With a partner, compare answers.

Form and Function

1 Do you have any experience?

Affirmative Statements

| I, you, we, they | have | **some** | experience. |
| he, she, (it) | has | | |

Negative Statements

| I, you, we, they | don't have | **any** | experience. |
| he, she, (it) | doesn't have | | |

Questions

| **Do** I, you, we, they | have | **any** | experience? |
| **Does** he, she, (it) | | | |

Examples

Karl needs **some** glasses.   Did you wash **any** glasses?

No, I did**n't** wash **any** glasses or plates.

Please give me **some** quarters. I do**n't** have **any** quarters. Do you want **any** other coins instead?

Practice 1

A. Listen. Circle the word you hear.

1. (some)   any   3. some   any   5. some   any

2. some   any   4. some   any   6. some   any

B. Work with a partner. Student A: Look at this page. Student B: Look at page 32. What does Carol have in her desk? Ask about the things below and write the answers in the box. Now look at Ben's desk. Answer your partner's questions.

books   pencils   papers   pens   notebooks

Example: A: Does Carol have any books in her desk? B: Yes, she has some books.

Work with a partner. Student B: Look at this page. Student A: Look at page 31.

Student B: Look at Carol's desk. Answer your partner's questions.

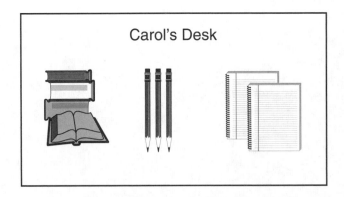

Carol's Desk

What does Ben have in his desk? Ask about the things below and write the answers in the box.

books   pencils   papers   pens   notebooks

Example: B: Does Ben have any books in his desk? A: No, he doesn't have any books.

```
Ben's Desk


        Notebooks
```

C. Fill in the correct word—*some* or *any*.

1. Do you have _____*any*_____ work experience?

2. I keep _____ application forms in the file cabinet.

3. I don't have _____ pens or pencils.

4. Elenora called about _____ jobs.

5. Did she go to _____ interviews?

6. Yes. She also had to fill out _____ applications.

7. We need _____ paper clips for these papers.

8. I didn't see _____ boxes in the supply room.

2 Are there any job openings?

Now	Yesterday
There is a newspaper.	**There was** a newspaper.
There is some money.	**There was** some money.
There are two newspapers.	**There were** two newspapers.
There are some files.	**There were** some files.

Examples

Is there a list of supplies?   Yes, **there's** a list on the bulletin board.
Are there any benefits?   No, **there aren't** any benefits.
Was there any overtime last week?   Yes, **there was** a lot of overtime.
Were there five boxes in the hall?   No, **there weren't** any boxes.

Practice 2

A. Listen. Circle the words you hear.

1. there is   (there was)
2. there is   there was
3. there is   there was

4. there are   there were
5. there are   there were
6. there are   there were

B. Match the parts of the sentences.

1. Is there

2. Are there

3. Was there

4. Were there

5. There's

6. There are

7. There was

8. There were

a. any jobs posted last week?

b. a red car here yesterday?

c. an application I can fill out now?

d. any job openings on the board today?

e. many people here last week.

f. a full-time job opening right now.

g. morning and evening hours available now.

h. an accident yesterday.

3 Would you like to fill out an application?

Would	I, you, he, she, we, they	like . . . ? like to . . . ?
Yes, No,	I, you, he, she, we, they I, you, he, she, we, they	would. wouldn't.
	I, you, he, she, we, they	would like . . . would like to . . .
	I'd, you'd, he'd, she'd, we'd, they'd	like . . . like to . . .

Examples

Would you like to go to dinner?
Would you like a cup of coffee?
I'd like to talk to you.

Would you like to come to a party at my place?
Would you like a drink?
I'd like a glass of water, please.

Practice 3

A. Listen. Circle the words you hear.

1. Do you like   (Would you like)
2. Do you like   Would you like
3. Would you like a   Would you like to

4. Would you like a   Would you like to
5. Do you like   Would you like
6. Would you like a   Would you like to

B. Complete the conversations below.

1. A: _____Would_____ you _____like to_____ come to my office for a second? I _____ to talk
   to you about something very interesting.
   B: Sure. I'll be right there.

2. A: When _____ you _____ come by for an interview?
   B: How about Thursday morning?

3. A: I _____ thank you for your help.
   B: You're welcome.

C. Choose one or two classmates. Invite your classmate(s) for coffee or tea after class.

> **Example:** A: Would you like to have a cup of tea after class?
> B: Sure! That's a good idea. OR: Sorry, not today. I'm busy.

Putting It to Work

1 Pair Work

Step 1. Listen. Circle the answers you think are better.

Interviewer: Please sit down.

A: OK.   B: Thank you.

Interviewer: I see on your application that you were a teacher.

A: Yes, I was.   B: That's right. I was a math teacher for three years.

Interviewer: Have you worked in a restaurant before?

A: No.   B: No, but I like to work with food. I cook for my family.

Interviewer: Why do you want to work in a restaurant?

A: I need a job.   B: I like to work with people, and I think I can use my math skills.

Interviewer: Do you have any questions about the job?

A: When is pay day?   B: Are there any training programs?

Step 2. With a partner, compare your answers. Then practice the conversation with your own answers.

2 Pair Work

Step 1. Listen to the dialogue. Then ask questions about the other jobs.

A: Are there any openings for a **secretary**?
B: Yes, there are.
A: What are the hours?
B: The hours are **9 to 5**.
A: What is the pay?
B: It's **$5.75** an hour.

A: Are there any benefits?
B: Yes, there are. There are **insurance and sick time.**
A: Is there **a training program?**
B: No, there isn't.

Step 2. Student A: Ask questions about the job. Fill in the answers on the chart.

Cook's helper

Hours _____   Pay _____

Benefits _____   Sick time _____

Insurance _____   Training _____

Vacation _____

> FILE CLERK
> 8:30–4:30
> $6.50/hour
> Benefits: insurance,
> vacation, and
> on-the-job training.

Now tell your partner about the job as a file clerk.

Student B: Tell your partner about this job:

```
Cook's Helper
2 P.M.–10 P.M.
$5.75/hour
No benefits
```

Now ask questions about the job below. Fill in the answers on the chart.

File Clerk

Hours	_____	Pay	_____
Benefits	_____	Sick time	_____
Insurance	_____	Training	_____
Vacation	_____		

With your partner, compare your answers.

3 Group/Class Work

Read these ideas. Check *Do* if you should do it for an interview. Check *Don't* if you shouldn't do it. Discuss with the group or class why.

DO	DON'T	
☐	☐	Come on time.
☐	☐	Look at the interviewer.
☐	☐	Give very short answers to questions.
☐	☐	Give long answers to questions.
☐	☐	Speak softly.
☐	☐	Speak clearly.

DO	DON'T	
☐	☐	Ask questions.
☐	☐	Dress neatly.
☐	☐	Thank the interviewer.
☐	☐	Prepare answers to questions.
☐	☐	Bring your children or friends with you.

4 Culture Work

Tran's interview is at 10:00. When should he arrive? What can he do if he is going to be late?

Unit 4
PAYDAY

Openers

Look at the picture. Point to these things and people:

check   cash   bank teller   ID

Where are they? What are they doing? What are they talking about?

1 Listen and Think

Listen to the conversations. Then circle the correct answers.

1. What does Binh want to do?   **a.** cash a check   **b.** write a check

2. Does Binh have an account at the bank?   **a.** yes   **b.** no

3. What does the teller need to see?   **a.** the paystub   **b.** some ID

4. Who needs to sign the check?   **a.** Binh   **b.** the bank teller

5. How much money does Binh get?   **a.** $166.49   **b.** $226.49

2 Talk to a Partner

Step 1.   Practice the conversation with a partner.

A: I'd like to cash this check.
B: Do you have some ID?
A: Yes, here's my **driver's license**.
B: Can you endorse the check, please?
   Here's your money. That's **$167.61**.
A: Thank you.

Step 2.   Change partners. Practice the conversation again. Use other types of ID and other amounts of money.

3 Read and Think

Step 1.   Look at the picture. Binh receives his paycheck every Friday.

Step 2.   Read the text.

Binh Van Tran is a machine operator at a printing factory. Binh gets paid every Friday. He receives a check and a paystub. Binh cashes the check at the bank, but he keeps the paystub. The paystub shows how many hours Binh worked and how much he is paid.

Binh usually works 40 hours a week. He gets $7.00 an hour. Binh's gross pay is $280.00. The company deducts money from his gross pay for taxes: federal, state, FICA (Social Security), and Medicare. Binh's paycheck is for $226.49. $226.49 is his net pay.

Step 3. Read the end of the text again. Find the the net pay on the paycheck and paystub below. Circle the amount.

0010092	Tran, Binh Van	075-09-3203	Deductions
Pay Period:	3/4/96–3/11/96		FICA 17.47
Hrs.	Base Rate	Gross Pay	Fed WH 24.96
40	7.00/hr.	280.00	State WH 6.99
			Medicare 4.09
			Net Pay 226.49

Acme Metal Co.   10092
1200 South Hadley Blvd.   March 18, 1996
Perkinsville, PA

Pay to the Order of _____ *Binh Van Tran* _____ $226.49

_____*****Two hundred twenty-six and 49/100*************_____

Chemical Trust Bank

Charles T. Morgan

Step 4. Read the vocabulary below. Then look at the paycheck and the stub again. Underline the words you know. Discuss the other words with the class.

Vocabulary

Paychecks

pay period   dates worked
base rate   money for each hour
hours   time worked
earnings   total money for work
deductions   money taken from pay for taxes and other items
taxes   money for state and federal governments
net pay   take-home money after taxes
gross pay   total money for work
FICA   Social Security taxes
Fed WH (abbreviation)   Federal taxes
State WH (abbreviation)   State taxes

Word Match

A. Match the examples with the meanings.

1. **35 hrs.** x $6.25/hr. = $218.75

2. **Jan. 7–Jan. 13, 1997**

3. 35 hrs. x **$6.25/hr.** = $218.75

4. 35 hrs. x $6.25/hr. = **$218.75**

5. $218.75 – FICA – taxes = **$192.25**

6. $218.75 – **FICA – taxes** = $192.25

a. gross pay _____

b. pay period _____

c. hours _____

d. deductions _____

e. base rate _____

f. net pay _____

B. Draw a line from the information on the paystub to the word.

Base rate   **Pay period**   **Gross pay**

0020564	Novak, Paulina	446-67-3987
	_____ : August 20, 1997–August 26, 1997	
Base rate		
$5.85/hr.	38 hrs.	$222.30
_____ :FICA 17.85 Fed WH 12.50 State WH 4.25 Medicare 3.75		$183.95

Net pay   **Deductions**   **Hours**

4 Put It in Writing

Step 1. Calculate these amounts for Mike's and Hannah's paychecks.

1. BASE RATE x HOURS = Mike's GROSS PAY

   $6.00/hr. x 40 hrs. = $ _____240.00_____

2. FICA + FED WH + STATE WH = Mike's DEDUCTIONS

   $14.88 + $12.06 + $3.38 = $ _____

3. GROSS PAY – DEDUCTIONS = Mike's NET PAY

   $240.00 – $30.32 = $ _____

4. BASE RATE x HOURS = Hannah's GROSS PAY

   $7.50/hr. x 30 hrs. = $ _____

5. FICA + FED WH + STATE WH = Hannah's DEDUCTIONS

   $12.87 + $15.06 + $4.15 = $ _____

6. GROSS PAY – DEDUCTIONS = Hannah's NET PAY

   $225.00 – $32.08 = $ _____

Step 2. With a partner, compare your answers.

5 Listen and Speak

Step 1. Listen to the conversation. Two employees are talking about their paychecks.

A: Hey, John. Did you get your paycheck?
B: Yes, I just got it. I'm going to cash it.
   But wait. There's something wrong.
A: Really?
B: Yes. There's a mistake. The hours
   aren't right.
A: It says **40 hours**.
B: Yes, but I worked **42 hours**.
A: You should tell your supervisor about it.
B: I should get an extra **$11.50**.

	Base Rate	Hours	Extra $
John	$5.75/hr.	40/42	$11.50
Carla	$5.90/hr.	32/35	$ ____
Anh	$6.50/hr.	30/34	$ ____

Step 2. Practice the conversation with a partner.

Step 3. Change partners. Practice again talking about other possible mistakes.

6 Read and Write

Step 1.   Read the paystub.

006567	Hector Garcia	032-55-4398	10/11/96–10/24/96	
HRS	Base Rate	Gross Pay	Deductions	
80	$6.05	$484.00	FICA	27.74
			FED WH	50.68
			STATE WH	14.19
			MEDICARE	6.49
			TOTAL DEDUCTIONS	99.10
			NET PAY	$384.90

Step 2.   Write the answers to the questions.

1. Whose check is this? _It's Hector Garcia's._

2. Does he get his check every week or every two weeks? _____

3. How many hours did he work? _____

4. How much does he get per hour? _____

5. What are his total earnings? _____

6. How much is his paycheck? _____

Step 3.   With a partner, compare your answers.

Form and Function

1 I'm going to cash my check.

I'm		I'm not		Am I	
You're		You aren't		Are you	
He's		He isn't		Is he	
She's	**going to** call later.	She isn't	**going to** call.	Is she	**going to** call us?
We're		We aren't		Are we	
They're		They aren't		Are they	

Examples

James **is going to** work late tonight.

Are you **going to** go to the bank this afternoon?

When are they **going to** finish the work?

He **isn't going to** play soccer tonight.

No, **I'm going to** go tomorrow.

They**'re going to** finish on Saturday.

Practice 1

A. Listen. Circle the word you hear.

1. are writing   (are going to write)

2. am calling   am going to call

3. is signing   is going to sign

4. is giving   is going to give

5. are paying   are going to pay

6. am waiting   am going to wait

B. Work with a partner. Ask questions. Student A: Look at this page. Student B: Look at page 44. Student A: Ask what Carol is going to do this week. Fill in the information.

> **Example:** A: What is Carol going to do on **Sunday**?
> B: She's going to **visit Maria**.

Sun.	Mon.	Tues.	Wed.	Thurs.	Fri.	Sat.
visit Maria						

Now look at John's plans for the week. Answer your partner's questions.

Sun.	Mon.	Tues.	Wed.	Thurs.	Fri.	Sat.
take the kids to the park	study	visit his brother	work late	go to the movies	write letters	watch TV

Student B: Look at Carol's plans for the week. Answer your partner's questions.

Example: A: What is Carol going to do on **Sunday**?
            B: She's going to **visit Maria**.

Sun.	Mon.	Tues.	Wed.	Thurs.	Fri.	Sat.
visit Maria	go to the library	bake a cake	take Mother to the clinic	shop for food	take a rest	work

Now ask what John is going to do this week. Fill in the information.

Sun.	Mon.	Tues.	Wed.	Thurs.	Fri.	Sat.

2 There's something wrong.

There's (There is)	**something** wrong.			
Is there	**anything** wrong?			
There **isn't** (is not)	**anything** wrong.	=	There's **nothing** wrong.	

Examples
There's **something** under that table.   No, there isn't. There's **nothing** under it.
Do you have **anything** for me?   No, I do**n't** have **anything**.

Practice 2

A. Listen. Circle the words you hear.

1. (something)   anything   nothing   4. something   anything   nothing

2. something   anything   nothing   5. something   anything   nothing

3. something   anything   nothing   6. something   anything   nothing

B. Fill in the missing words: *something, anything, nothing*.

1. Is there _____*anything*_____ wrong with the computer?

   No, there's _____ wrong with it.

2. There's _____ wrong with the sink!

   Is there _____ I can do to help?

3. There's _____ wrong with my telephone.

   Is there _____ wrong with yours?

4. Is _____ wrong?

   Yes, there's _____ wrong with my paycheck.

C. Work with a partner. Ask questions with *anything*.

Student A: Ask about the things in the kitchen. Check the answers.

Example: A: Is there anything wrong with the **vacuum?**
B: **Yes, there's something wrong. It's broken.**

The Office

	Something is wrong.	Nothing is wrong.
vacuum	✓	
stove		
refrigerator		
sink		
television		
window		

Now, look at the office. Answer your partner's questions.

Student B: Look at the kitchen. Answer your partner's questions.

Example: Is there anything wrong with the **sink?**
Yes, there's something wrong. It's broken.

	Something is wrong.	Nothing is wrong.
computer	✓	
photocopier		
telephone		
table		
stapler		
door		

The Kitchen

Ask about the things in the office. Check the answers.

With your partner, compare your answers.

D. Use the information in your chart. Write questions and answers. Follow the model above.

1. _Is there anything wrong with the_ _____ computer?

  Yes, _____. It's broken.

2. _____ photocopier?

  Yes, _____. It's broken.

3. _____ telephone?

  Yes, _____. It's broken.

4. _____ table?

  Yes, _____. It's broken.

5. _____ stapler?

  Yes, _____. It's broken.

6. _____ door?

  Yes, _____. It's broken.

Putting It to Work

1 Pair Work

Step 1. Listen. With a partner, fill in the missing amounts on the paystub and check.

```
0010092          Chavez, Ramon      214-64-6772
Pay Period: 3/4/96–3/11/96
Hrs.                          Base Rate              Gross Pay
_____                  _____           _____

Deductions
FICA _____   Fed WH _____   State WH _____   Medicare _____
                                                            Net Pay _____
```

```
Acme Metal Co.                                              10092
1200 South Hadley Blvd.          March 18, 1996
Perkinsville, PA

Pay to the Order of _____ Ramon Chavez _____ $ _____

_____

Chemical Trust Bank
                              _____ Charles T. Morgan _____
```

Step 2. With another pair of classmates, compare your answers.

2 Pair Work

Step 1. Listen to the conversation.

A: How many hours did Ramon work?
B: He worked 20 hours.
A: What's the base rate?
B: Seven dollars an hour.
A: What are the dates for the pay period?

B: May 14 through May 20, 1997.
A: How much is the gross pay?
B: $140.00.
A: How much is the FICA?
B: $6.50.

Step 2. Student A: Ask questions. Fill in the blanks. Calculate the gross and net pay.

```
0010092          Chavez, Ramon      214-64-6772
Pay Period: _____
Hrs.                          Base Rate              Gross Pay
                              $7.00
_____                                         _____

Deductions
FICA _____   Fed WH _____   State WH 3.38   Medicare _____
Health Insurance 10.25                                Net Pay _____
```

Listen to the conversation.

A: How many hours did Ramon work?

B: He worked 20 hours.

A: What's the base rate?

B: Seven dollars an hour.

A: What are the dates for the pay period?

B: May 14 through May 20, 1997.

A: How much is the gross pay?

B: $140.00.

A: How much is the FICA?

B: $6.50.

Student B: Ask questions. Fill in the blanks. Calculate the gross and net pay.

0010092 Chavez, Ramon 214-64-6772		
Pay Period: 5/14/97–5/20/97		
Hrs. 20	Base Rate _____	Gross Pay $140.00
Deductions		
FICA $6.50 Fed WH 12.06 State WH _____		Medicare 3.48
Health Insurance _____		Net Pay _____

Step 3. Talk to another pair of classmates and compare your answers.

3 Group/Class Work

Step 1. Read about these workers. In a group, calculate their net pay.

Name	Eduardo	Marina	Paul	Fatima
How paid	check	cash	check	check
Gross pay	$335.00	$300.00	$335.00	$350.00
Taxes	$ 65.00	_____	$ 65.00	$ 70.00
Other deductions	$ 10.50 health ins.		_____	$ 10.50; $12.25 health ins.; retirement
Net Pay	$ _____	$ _____	$ _____	$ _____

Step 2. Discuss the advantages and disadvantages of each worker's pay. Do you agree or disagree with the other students in your group?

Step 3. Tell the class your opinions.

4 Culture Work

With the class, discuss this question: How do employees receive their pay in your country?

Unit 5
TEAMWORK

Openers

Look at the picture. Point to these things:

conveyor belt   forklift   uniform
hard hat   switch   lever

Where are they? What are they talking about? What are they doing?

1 Listen and Think

Listen to the conversation and number the jobs in the correct order.

_____ put the boxes in a pile   __*1*__ fill the machine with glue

_____ pack the books in the boxes   _____ use the forklift to move the boxes to
                                          the loading area

_____ check the book covers

2 Talk to a Partner

Step 1. Practice the conversation with a partner.

A: Good morning. Woodsville Printing Company. Can I help you?
B: Yes. This is Peter Kalas. I'm sorry, but **I can't come to work today**.
A: I'm sorry to hear that. What's the matter?
B: **My son is sick**. I have to **take him to the clinic**.
A: All right. I'll tell your supervisor.
B: Thank you.

Step 2. Change partners. Practice calling in sick and late.

3 Read and Think

Step 1. Look at the picture. Lana Martin works at a printing company, and today, one of the employees is not at work.

Step 2. Read the text.

Lana Martin is a supervisor at the Woodsville Printing Company. She plans the work schedule and assigns jobs to the workers in her group. Today Peter Kalas is not at work. Peter usually works on the conveyor belt. He checks the covers of the books. Lana is going to change the work assignments.

In the morning before the work shift begins, Lana tells the group about changes in the job assignments. Today Fran and Larry have extra work, but everyone in the group helps out.

Step 3. Look at the work schedule below. What parts does Lana have to change? With a partner, circle those parts of the schedule.

Fran	Do 10 lots of books (*ECG Company Policy Manual*) Check print	Do 15 more lots of books Check print
Larry	Print 30 lots of books (*Hermann's Tax Guide*)	Check print
Peter	Do 35 lots of covers (*ECG Company Policy Manual*) Check covers	Do 30 lots of covers (*Hermann's Tax Guide*) Check covers

Step 4. With a group, discuss these questions: Can Fran and Larry do all of Peter's work? Does Lana need to find someone else? Does Lana need to help? Do you have any other ideas? Which choice do you prefer?

Vocabulary

Job Words and Actions

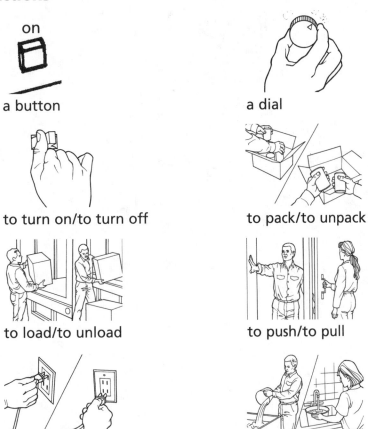

on

a button

a dial

to turn on/to turn off

to pack/to unpack

to load/to unload

to push/to pull

to plug in/to unplug

to empty/to fill

Word Match

A. Match the action with the situation.

1. The stove is on fire!
2. There's no water in the bucket.
3. This bag is too full.
4. Put these boxes on the truck.
5. Take the books out of the box.
6. Press the button to start it.

a. Load them.
b. Unpack them.
c. Turn it off!
d. Fill it.
e. Turn it on.
f. Empty it.

B. Draw a line from the word to the machine part.

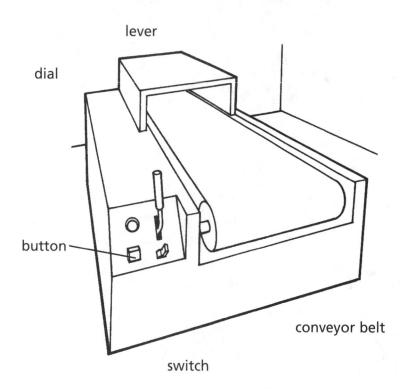

lever

dial

button

conveyor belt

switch

4 Put It in Writing

Answer these questions.

1. How do I start this?

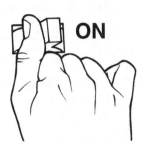

_____

2. How do I turn it off?

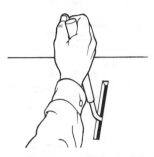

_____

3. How do I slow it down?

_____

4. How do I stop it?

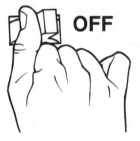

_____

5 Listen and Speak

Step 1. **Listen. Practice the conversation with a partner.**

A: Can you work on the **conveyor belt**?
B: Sure. What do I have to do?
A: First **turn on the machine**.
B: OK.
A: Then **check the book covers**.
B: **Check the book covers**.
A: And then **put the books in the boxes**.
B: **Put the books in the boxes**. All right.

Step 2. **Change partners. Practice giving directions to these workers.**

Fran: conveyor belt
  • turn on machine
  • check book covers
  • put books in boxes

Mark: loading dock
  • count boxes
  • load boxes on truck
  • write the number on the order form

Hung-ju: binding machine
  • turn off machine
  • empty the glue
  • sweep the floor

6 Read and Write

Step 1.   Read the instructions.

Washer Instructions

Please follow instructions carefully.

1. Arrange clothes inside the washer. Caution: Do not overload.
2. Turn the dial to select water temperature.
3. Add laundry detergent.
4. Pour bleach into proper container.
5. Close the lid.
6. Insert $0.75 in the machine slot. (Quarters only.)
7. Push in coin slot slowly to start machine.
8. Do not open until washer has completed the cycle.

Step 2.   Write the answers to the questions.

1. Where do you put the clothes? *Inside the washer.*

2. How do you select the water temperature? _____

3. How much does it cost to wash the clothes? _____

4. Does the detergent go in before or after the bleach? _____

5. How do you start the machine? _____

6. Can you use dimes in this machine? _____

Step 3.   With a partner, compare answers.

Form and Function

1 Do you like to work at night?

	I, you, we, they he, she, (it)	**like to** **likes to**	work at night.		like to
	I, you, we, they he, she, (it)	**don't like to** **doesn't like to**	work at night.		begin to want to
Do **Does**	I, you, we, they he, she, (it)	**like to**	work at night?		decide to need to forget to
When do **When does**	I, you, we, they he, she, (it)	**like to**	work?		try to hate to

Examples

Karl **needs to** talk to the supervisor.
Do you **want to** get some coffee?

Don't **forget to** pick up your check!
We **decided to** go to New York.

Practice 1

A. Listen. Circle the words you hear.

1. want   (want to)

2. forget   forget to

3. likes   likes to

4. try   try to

5. begin   begin to

6. needs   needs to

B. Fill in the correct words.

forgot to   try to   hate to
wants to   begin to   decided to

1. Where did you take your vacation?

   I ___decided to___ go to Florida.

2. Do you want to play football?

   Not really. I _____ play football.

3. Did you pack all the boxes?

   No, we're going to _____ do it now.

4. Did you remember to wash the dishes?

   Sorry, I _____ wash them.

5. When do you start your job at the factory?

   I _____ work there next Monday.

6. What's Mike planning to do tonight?

   He _____ go to the movies.

C. Ask three classmates about their likes and dislikes. Write the answers below.

What do you like to do on Saturdays?
What do you hate to do?

Name	like to	hate to
1.		
2.		
3.		

2 I have to take my son to the clinic.

Present	Past	Present	Past
I **have to** . . .		I **need to** . . .	
You **have to** . . .		You **need to** . . .	
He **has to** . . .		He **needs to** . . .	
She **has to** . . .	**had to** . . .	She **needs to** . . .	needed to . . .
We **have to** . . .		We **need to** . . .	
They **have to** . . .		They **need to** . . .	

Examples

She **has to** <u>sweep</u> the kitchen.
I **need to** <u>wash</u> this counter.
Did you **have to** <u>fill</u> out a report?

What do you **have to** <u>do</u>?

No, we didn't **have to**.

Practice 2

A. Listen. Circle the word(s) you hear.

1. (have)   have to

2. need   need to

3. has   has to

4. need   need to

5. had   had to

6. needed   needed to

7. had   had to

8. needed   needed to

B. Fill in the correct forms of the verbs.

1. Paula and Kim _____*have to*_____ (have/have to) take the bus to work.

2. Mary _____ (has/has to) go to the dentist today.

3. We _____ (have/have to) a new car.

4. Did you _____ (have/have to) wash the car?

5. I _____ (need/need to) talk to the teacher.

6. John _____ (needs/needs to) some glasses.

7. Did you _____ (need/need to) work overtime?

8. The supervisor _____ (needed/needed to) more copies of the schedule.

C. Ask your partner questions about the work schedule.

Student A: Find out what these workers have to do today. Fill in the missing information on the schedule.

> **Example:** A: Is Daniele **operating the forklift** today?
> B: No, she isn't. She has to **check the book covers** today.

Work Schedule: Section D		
Workers	**Yesterday**	**Today?**
Daniele	operate the forklift	*check the book covers*
Miguel	count books	
Joe	pack boxes	
George	work on the conveyor belt	
Hung-ju	check the book covers	
Rennie	count boxes	

Now answer your partner's questions about yesterday's schedule.

> **Example:** B: Did Daniele **check the book covers** yesterday?
> A: No, she didn't. She had to **operate the forklift**.

Student B: Answer your partner's questions about today's schedule.

> **Example:** A: Is Daniele **operating the forklift** today?
> B: No, she isn't. She has to **check the book covers** today.

Work Schedule: Section D		
Workers	**Yesterday**	**Today?**
Daniele	*operate the forklift*	check the book covers
Miguel		count boxes
Joe		operate the forklift
George		pack boxes
Hung-ju		count books
Rennie		work on the conveyor belt

Now ask questions about yesterday's schedule. Fill in the missing information.

> **Example:** A: Did Daniele **check the book covers** yesterday?
> B: No, she didn't. She had to **operate the forklift**.

With your partner, compare your answers.

D. Read the directions for the photocopier below. The directions are in the wrong order. With a partner, put the directions in the right order. Then tell your partner what you have to do and when.

> **Example:** First, you have to _____.
>
> Then you have to _____.

_____ Press Start.

_____ Take the copy out of the tray.

_____ Put the original in the feeder.

_____ Select the paper size.

feeder

tray

button for
paper size

Putting It to Work

1 Pair Work

Step 1. Listen. Number the tasks in the correct order.

_____	Put a filter in the filter holder.
_____	Pour a pot of water into the top of the coffee maker.
_____	Wait for the pot to be full before removing.
_1_	Turn the machine on.
_____	Place the coffee pot on the burner under the filter holder.
_____	Put one bag of coffee into the filter.
_____	Slide the filter holder into place on the machine.

Step 2. With a partner, compare your answers.

Step 3. Role-play. Give instructions using your answers.

2 Pair Work

Step 1. With a partner, listen and complete the instructions.

COPY MACHINE XZ-2000

Instructions

1. Lift ___*top*___ of the copy machine.

2. Place original _____ face-down on the machine.

3. Select the size of the paper: letter or legal.

4. Put the _____ down.

5. Enter the number of copies to be made.

6. Press the _____ button.

7. When the machine is finished, remove the original page.

8. Take copies from the rack on the _____ .

See manual for more detailed instructions and product specifications.

Step 2. Check your answers. Change partners. Ask another classmate for instructions.

Example: A: What do I do first?
B: Lift the top of the copy machine.

Step 3. Change roles. Answer your partner's questions.

3 Group/Class Work

Step 1. With a group, look at the office schedule below. Each student in the group takes one of the roles below. Except for the role of Alice. Alice won't be at work today.

You all have to do some of Alice's work. What changes do you need to make to the schedule? Discuss this question with your group.

Monday, October 5			
Jim	**Alice**	**Bob**	**Freda**
Distribute the mail	Read 100 letters	Phone 70 customers	Put labels on 100 envelopes
Take the mail to the Post Office	Answer 100 letters	Take orders from customers	Put 100 letters into envelopes and address them
Make 1,000 photocopies	Write 20 more letters to new customers	Phone 35 stores	Put 10 photocopies into each envelope
		Write a report on each store	

Step 2. Write a new schedule on a separate sheet of paper.

Step 3. What changes did you make? Tell the class.

4 Culture Work

Omar is a highly skilled employee, and he's a new worker in Lana's department. Omar is unhappy because his boss is a woman. He doesn't want to work under a woman. What can Lana's team do? How can they discuss this situation with Omar?

Step 1. Work with a group. Choose a team leader, a team recorder, and a team reporter. Read the possible solutions below and add your own ideas.

Step 2. Rank the solutions (including your own ideas) with numbers in order of preference. Discuss any disagreements.

_____ Each member of the department can talk to Omar separately. Each person can tell Omar that Lana is a good supervisor.

_____ The others can stop talking to Omar. Eventually, he will learn to accept women in positions of authority.

_____ As a group, the others can tell Omar to relax. After all, men and women can work well together.

_____ As a group, the others can tell Omar he is wrong. After all, women can do everything men can do. Men have to respect women's authority.

Step 3. Your team reporter will report your ideas to the class.

Unit 6
SUPPLY ORDERS

Openers

Look at the picture. Point to these things:

entrance   stairs   supply room
emergency exit   loading dock   cafeteria

Peter

Where are they? What are they talking about?

1 Listen and Think

Listen to the conversation. Then draw a line on the illustration above to show where Peter goes. Circle the things he needs to get.

2 Talk to a Partner

Step 1. Practice the conversations with a partner.

> Peter: I'm going to the **supply room**. Do
> you need anything?
> Lana: Would you pick up **my clipboard**?
> Peter: All right. I'll be back in a little while.

> Lana: Peter, can you get me **my keys**?
> Peter: **Your keys**? Sure, where are they?
> Lana: I think they're **in the cafeteria**.
> Peter: I'll go check.

Step 2. Change partners. Practice following and giving directions.

3 Read and Think

Step 1. Look at the picture. Marco gets supplies for the other employees.

Step 2. Read the text.

Marco works in the supply room at the printing company. His job is to get the other employees tools and supplies for work. Every day, the employees come and ask for supplies like paper, glue, ink, erasers, and notebooks. Marco asks them to fill out a request form. He needs to know a lot of information— like the supplies needed, the number of items, and the department. Usually Marco can just give the employees their supplies. But sometimes, he has to order the supplies from another company. With so many supply orders, Marco is very busy.

Step 3. Look at the vocabulary on page 63. Marco orders tools and supplies like the items in the pictures.

Vocabulary

Tools and Supplies

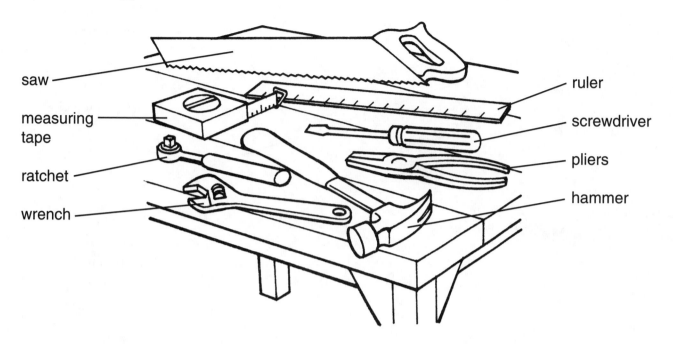

saw

measuring tape

ratchet

wrench

ruler

screwdriver

pliers

hammer

screws

nails

bolts

tacks

nuts

washers

wire

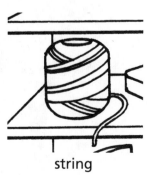

string

Word Match

A. Listen. Match the tool with the place.

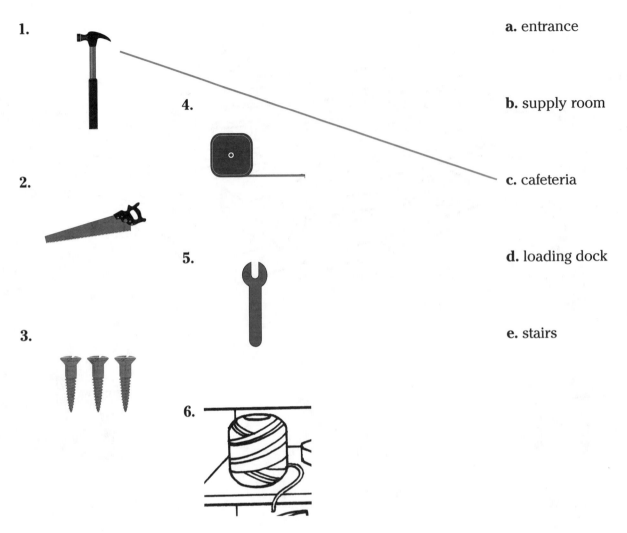

1.

4.

a. entrance

b. supply room

2.

c. cafeteria

5.

d. loading dock

3.

e. stairs

6.

B. Count the supplies. Then write the number next to the name of the items.

Item	Quantity
nuts	
washers	
nails	
screws	
bolts	

4 Put It in Writing

Answer the questions.

1. Where are the keys? _The keys are on the chair._

2. Is the saw on the shelves? _____

3. Where is the clipboard? _____

4. Is there a wrench on the table? _____

5. How many boxes of paper are there? _____

6. Where is the screwdriver? _____

5 Listen and Speak

Step 1.   Listen.

A: I need some computer disks.
B: Oh.
A: Would you go to the supply room and get some?
B: Some **disks**? Sure. How many do you need?
A: About **three boxes**. Oh, we need some **glue**, too.
B: All right, **three boxes of disks and some glue**. I'll be right back.

Step 2.   Practice the conversation with a partner.

Step 3.   Change partners. Practice asking for other supplies.

6 Read and Write

Step 1. Read the supply request form.

REQUEST FOR SUPPLIES		
DEPT: *Production*		DATE: *3/14/97*
Quantity	**Item**	**Description**
1. ✓ 1	Measuring tape	20' long
2. ✓ 3 boxes	Nails	1/2"
3. 5 coils	Wire	welding 5/16"
4. ✓ 2 boxes	Garbage bags	
5. ✓ 4 cans	White paint	5-gallon cans
6. ✓ 10	Paintbrushes	2"

Step 2. Write the answers to the questions.

1. When were these supplies ordered? ___*March 14, 1997*_____

2. How many measuring tapes are ordered? _____

3. What color paint is ordered? _____

4. What supplies come in boxes? _____

5. Do you think they have 5 coils of wire? _____

6. Which supply comes in 5-gallon cans? _____

Step 3. With a partner, compare answers.

Form and Function

1 Would you pick up my clipboard?

Can you call me tonight?	**Would you call** me tonight?
Can you hand me the tools?	**Would you hand** me the tools?

Examples

A: **Would you come** here a minute? B: Sure.   A: **Would you clean** this room first? B: Yes, I will.
A: **Would you work** with Frank today? B: All right.

Practice 1

A. Listen. Circle the word you hear.

1. would   (can)
2. would   can
3. would   can

4. would   can
5. would   can
6. would   can

B. Work with a partner. Student A: Look at this page only. Student B: Look at page 68. Ask politely for the things marked A on the chart. Answer your partner's questions.

Example: B: Would you give me **a ruler**, please?
            A: Sure. There's **one on the table**. You can take it.

Tools and Supplies	Where?
B. A ruler	one on the table
A. A can of paint	
B. A key to the supply room	one on the hook
A. A box of 12-D nails	
B. A box of envelopes	one on the top shelf
A. A can of paint thinner	

Work with a partner. Student B: Look at this page only. Student A: Look at page 67. Ask politely for the things marked B on the chart. Answer your partner's questions.

Tools and Supplies	Where?
B. A ruler	
A. A can of paint	one in the supply room
B. A key to the supply room	
A. A box of 12-D nails	one on my desk
B. A box of envelopes	
A. A can of paint thinner	one on the bottom shelf

B. Look at the pictures. Circle the command you would use for these situations.

1.

    a. Would you call 911?

    (**b.** Call 911!)

2.

    a. Would you get me some coffee?

    b. Get me some coffee!

3.

    a. Would you put on a hard hat?

    b. Put on a hard hat!

4.

    a. Would you take these to the office?

    b. Take these papers to the office!

2 I'll be back in a little while.

I You He She **will** **work hard.** We ('ll) They	I You He She **won't** **be** at work. We (will not) They	**Will**	I you he she **arrive** soon? we they?

Examples

Will you **be** in class tonight?
When will we **get** paid?
Where will they **stay**?

No, I **won't**. **I'll be** at the library.
On Friday.
They**'ll stay** at my sister's house.

Practice 2

A. Listen. Circle *will* or *won't*. Then draw a line to the action.

1. (will)   won't   **a.** play

2. will   won't   **b.** be at work

3. will   won't   **c.** cash the check

4. will   won't   **d.** go to the store

5. will   won't   **e.** arrive on time

6. will   won't   **f.** be late

B. Work with a partner. Ask questions with *will*. Student A: Look at this page only. Student B: Look at page 70. Complete the chart.

Example: A: Where will **Ramon** go on vacation?
B: He'll go **to Florida**.

Who?	Where?	When?	How?
Ramon	*to Florida*		
Marie		next month	
George and Diane	to Mexico		by car
(you)			

**Work with a partner. Ask questions with *will*. Student B: Look at this page only.
Student A: Look at page 69. Complete the chart.**

Example: A: Where will **Ramon** go on vacation?
B: He'll go **to Florida**.

Who?	Where?	When?	How?
Ramon	to Florida	in April	by plane
Marie	to Canada		by bus
George and Diane		in two weeks	
(you)			

3 There aren't any disks here, and there aren't any in the other room, either.

Affirmative	Negative
Eva **works** very hard, and Jan **does, too**.	Carrie **doesn't work** hard, and Joan **doesn't either**.

Practice 3

A. Listen. Circle True or False.

1. Sergei is from Moscow. (T) F
2. Luz lives in Los Angeles. T F
3. Kathy doesn't drive. T F
4. Cyndi doesn't like sports. T F
5. Ron doesn't have a stapler. T F
6. Fred works as a waiter. T F

B. Combine the sentences below.

1. Dan is on our team. June is on our team.

   Dan is on our team, and June is, too.

2. Terry doesn't take supply orders. Mary doesn't take supply orders.

   _____

3. Radio City doesn't sell computers. Our store doesn't sell computers.

   _____

4. Doug works the night shift. Jeff works the night shift.

   _____

1 Pair Work

Step 1. Listen. Fill out the missing information on the supply request form.

Request for Supplies		
DEPT: Production		DATE: _____

	Quantity	Item
1.	1	_____
2.	_____	Tacks
3.	5	_____
4.	_____	Pliers
5.	4 balls	_____
6.		Rulers

Step 2. With a partner, compare your answers. Then ask and answer questions about the order.

2 Pair Work

Step 1. With a partner, listen to the conversation and note the supplies and quantities on the checklist below.

Checklist	
Item	Quantity in Stock
1. Washers	_____
2. Paint	_____
3. Envelopes	_____
4. Tacks	_____
5. String	_____
6. Glue	_____
7. Notebooks	_____
8. Wire	_____
9. Paint trays	_____

Supply Request Form	
DEPT: Production DATE: 3/14/97	
Item	Quantity
1. _____ _____	
2. _____ _____	
3. _____ _____	
4. _____ _____	

Step 2. You can request only four items. Fill out the supply request form. Which supplies do you really need? With your partner, order those supplies.

Example:

A: Do we really need string?
B: No, we don't.

A: Do we need paint?
B: Yes, we need 10 cans.

3 Group/Class Work

Step 1.   With a group, look at the pictures. Decide which tools and supplies they might need. Make a list for each job.

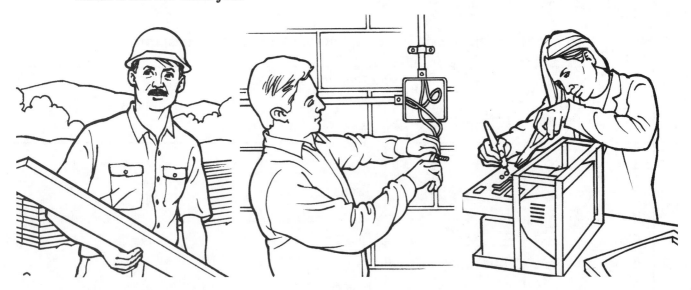

Step 2.   Practice requesting the tools on your list.

Step 3.   Read your list to the class.

4 Culture Work

Read the sentences below. When do you use a polite form or a command?

Don't smoke in here!   Sign this paper!
Can you stop smoking?   Can you sign this paper?
Would you please not smoke in here?   Would you sign this paper for me please?

How do you ask other workers to do things?
How do you ask an employer?
Can you think of other times when you use different forms for requests?

Unit 7
WRITE IT DOWN

Openers

Look at the picture. Point to these things:

time card   paperwork   computer screen

Where are they? What are they talking about?

1 Listen and Think

Listen to the conversation and answer the questions.

1. What did Marco forget to sign?   **a.** the inventory   **b.** the time sheet

2. Where does he need to go?   **a.** to the supply room   **b.** to the office

3. Who does he need to see?   **a.** Julio   **b.** Ellen

4. When will Marco get paid?   **a.** next Monday   **b.** Friday

5. How many hours did he work?   **a.** 32   **b.** 42

2 Talk to a Partner

Step 1. Practice the conversations with a partner.

A: I need your **time sheet**.
B: OK. When do you need it?
A: **This afternoon**.
B: OK. It'll be ready by then.

A: When do you need the **inventory**?
B: **Today at 5:00**.
A: OK. I'll work on it now.

Inventory Sheet
Time Card
Supply Form
Schedule

tomorrow
THIS AFTERNOON

next Monday
at 2:00

Step 2. Change partners. Practice asking about paperwork and times.

3 Read and Think

Step 1. Look at the picture. Marco has a lot of paperwork.

Step 2. Read the text.

"Paperwork! Too many papers!" Marco is working on the inventory for the supply room. He fills out these papers every three months. It takes a lot of time to count and list all of the items in the room. But Marco knows where everything is and how much he has. The papers help him get the supplies for the other workers.

In addition to inventories and time sheets, there are schedules every week. Every month there's a report. And every year an evaluation. "Paperwork! Too many papers!"

Step 3. Look at the vocabulary on page 75. Then read the text again.

Step 4. Look at Marco's time sheet. Find the overtime hours and circle them. Calculate the total hours for 3/13 and 3/16. Calculate the total for the week.

Waxwood Printing and Binding
Time Sheet

Employee No.: 330-7
Name: Marco Hernandez
Dept: Supplies

Period ending: 3/17/97
Supervisor: Kim Moodey

	Regular Hours	Overtime	Vacation	Holiday Hours	Sick Hours	Total
3/13	8	1				___
3/14	8					8
3/15	8					8
3/16	8	2				___
3/17				8		8
Total						___

Step 5. Marco makes $10.00 an hour. For overtime, he earns time and a half, or 1½ times his normal wage. How much money did he make in overtime? Find the answer with a partner.

Vocabulary

Records and Inventory

deadline the day and time when a paper needs to be finished
inventory a total counting of items and supplies in a business
schedule a plan that shows when, who, and where things are happening
delivery schedule a paper that shows when things will arrive
work schedule a paper that shows when people work
checklist a paper that lists tasks or things that need to be done
weekly report a paper that tells what was done in a week

Dates

Month / Day / Year
June 15, 1997

Month / Day / Year
6 / 15 / 97

Month / Day
September 3

Month / Day
9 / 3

Word Match

A. Draw a line. Match the dates.

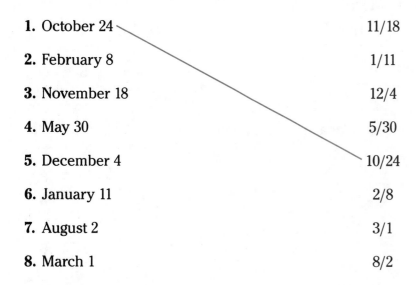

1. October 24   11/18

2. February 8   1/11

3. November 18   12/4

4. May 30   5/30

5. December 4   10/24

6. January 11   2/8

7. August 2   3/1

8. March 1   8/2

B. Listen. Circle the dates.

1. (6/15)   6/12   12/6   4. 11/1   9/9   11/5

2. 8/9   9/18   8/19   5. 6/2   7/2   7/7

3. 3/23   2/13   2/23   6. 4/30   3/13   4/3

C. Fill in the missing words.

deadline	delivery schedule	inventory
schedule	checklist	

1. Marco is counting supplies for the ___*inventory*_____.

2. Lana is preparing a list to tell people when they work next week.

   She's making a _____.

3. The paper needs to be in the office at 5:00. 5:00 is the _____.

4. Each worker has a _____ to make sure all the work is done.

5. At the loading dock, there is a _____ to show when

   more supplies will arrive.

4 Put It in Writing

Look at the calendar. Then write the dates on the forms.

	From	To

1.

SEPTEMBER
SUNDAY	MONDAY	TUESDAY	WEDNESDAY	THURSDAY	FRIDAY	SATURDAY
	1	2	3	4	5	6
7	8	9	10	11	12	13
14	15	16	17	18	19	20
21	22	23	24	25	26	27
28	29	30	31			

_____ – _____

2.

May
SUNDAY	MONDAY	TUESDAY	WEDNESDAY	THURSDAY	FRIDAY	SATURDAY
						1
2	3	4	5	6	7	8
9	10	11	12	13	14	15
16	17	18	19	20	21	22
23 30	24	25	26	27	28	29

_____ – _____

3.

JANUARY
SUNDAY	MONDAY	TUESDAY	WEDNESDAY	THURSDAY	FRIDAY	SATURDAY
						1
2	3	4	5	6	7	8
9	10	11	12	13	14	15
16	17	18	19	20	21	22
23 30	24	25	26	27	28	29

_____ – _____

4.

JUNE 1997
SUNDAY	MONDAY	TUESDAY	WEDNESDAY	THURSDAY	FRIDAY	SATURDAY
1	2	3	4	5	6	7
8	9	10	11	12	13	14
15	16	17	18	19	20	21
22	23	24	25	26	27	28
29	30					

_____ – _____

5 Listen and Speak

Step 1. Listen to the conversation.

> A: We have to do the **inventory this week**.
>   When's a good time for you?
> B: **Today's** OK.
> A: **Tomorrow's** better for me. I have too
>   much work **today**.
> B: OK, but I want to do the **smaller boxes** first.
>   The **larger ones** are easy. We can do them fast.
> A: Fine.

Step 2. Practice the conversation with a partner.

**Step 3. Role-play a similar conversation. Decide on a time
to do the other things. What do you want to do first?
Tell your partner your preferences.**

6 Read and Write

Step 1. Read the supply transmittal form.

Supply Transmittal Notice

Item/Size	Code No.	Quantity	Unit Cost
Phillips head screwdrivers, 7 inch	90446-XA	20	3.59
Electrical tape, 3 inches wide	8553-RE	10 rolls	4.59
Computer disks, 3½ inch, high-density	24635-Z	5 boxes	7.99
Copy paper, 8½ x 11	45688-NJ	4 boxes	25.00
Copy paper, 11 x 17	45689-NJ	4 boxes	31.00
Toner cartridges, large	1896-EG	5	50.00

Important! Keep this TOTAL for your records: _____

Transmitted to Department: __Maintenance_____ Date: __10/21/96__

Recipient: __Leslie Barker__ Supervisor (if necessary): _____

Step 2. Write the answers to the questions.

1. What is the date on the form? _____

2. What are the supplies on the form? _____

_____

3. How much electrical tape did the company order? _____

4. What's the code for the Phillips head screwdrivers? _____

5. What's the unit price of the toner cartridges? _____

6. What is the total cost of the computer disks? _____

Step 3. With a partner, figure out the total cost of all of the items together. Multiply the quantity by the unit cost. Then add all of the figures.

Step 4. With another pair of classmates, compare answers.

1 I want to do the smaller boxes first.

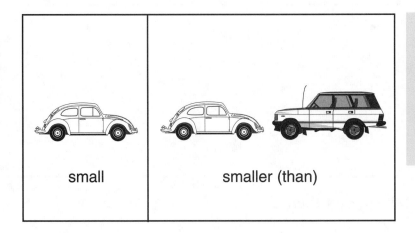

small   smaller (than)

large	larg**er**
big	big**ger**
late	late**r**
heavy	heav**ier**
good	**better**
bad	**worse**

Examples

The printing company is in a **large** building. The building is **larger than** the hospital.

Practice 1

A. Listen. Circle the word you hear.

1. (big)   bigger   **4.** good   better

2. heavy   heavier   **5.** short   shorter

3. easy   easier   **6.** tall   taller

B. Fill in the correct form of the adjective.

1. This report is very _____*long*_____ (long).

2. This form is _____ (long) than the time sheet form.

3. This is the _____ (good) job for me.

4. The new machine is _____ (heavy) than the old one.

5. This lesson is very _____ (hard).

6. Do you have a _____ (small) screwdriver than this one?

C. Work with a partner. Talk about a place you lived before and the place you live now. Use words like *bigger*, *smaller*, *better*, *easier*.

	Where I live now	Where I lived before
bigger smaller prettier better nicer cleaner easier		

D. Which place do you like better? Tell your partner.

2 You must sign your time sheet.

	I, you, he, she, we, they	**must** **must not**	sign	the form.
Must	I, you, he, she, we, they		sign	the form?
What must	I, you, he, she, we, they		sign?	

Examples

The supervisor **must sign** the form.
She **must not touch** that wire!

Must we **do** this inventory today?
We **must not forget** to sign in!

Practice 2

A. Listen. Check *must* or *must not*.

	You must	You must not	
1.	✓	_____	use the back door.
2.	_____	_____	eat on the loading dock.
3.	_____	_____	smoke in the building.
4.	_____	_____	write on this paper.
5.	_____	_____	leave the boxes here.
6.	_____	_____	go into this room.

B. Look at the pictures. Complete the sentences.

1. You must _____.

2. You must not _____.

C. Talk to a friend about things you must do and must not do at work or at school.

3 Could you help me for a second?

Get the broom!

Could you **get** the mop?

Examples
Could you **help** me?
Could you **lift** that box?

I'm sorry, I **can't** right now.
Sure.

Practice 3

A. Listen. Circle the word you hear.

1. (can)   could   3. can   could   5. can   could

2. can   could   4. can   could   6. can   could

B. Write a polite command for these actions.

1.

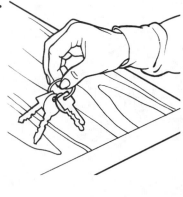

_____

_____

2.

_____

_____

3.

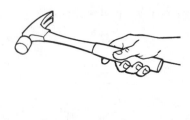

_____

_____

4.

_____

_____

C. Role-play. With a partner, choose one of the tasks below. Ask for help with the task. Change roles.

- Fill out a time sheet
- Fill out a supply request form
- Fill out a W-4 form

- Fill out a tax form
- Fill out a job application form
- Fill out an insurance form

Example:　A: Could you help me with this **time sheet**? I need to fill it out.
　　　　　　B: Sure. Just put **your name** right here. And what's **your employee number**?
　　　　　　A: **70301**.

Here are some details for some of the forms:

- your employee number
- your date of birth

- your name
- your address

- the supply item
- the supply code

1 Pair Work

Step 1. Listen and fill out the work order schedule.

Jake's Auto Repair						
Work Orders for: 7/22					
Workers: Nancy, Carl, Jake					
Date	Time in	Name	Problem	Worker	Garage #
7/22		Olson	tune up		
		Carnes	starter		
		Lindsey	oil change		
		Tran	exhaust		
		Silva	brakes		

Step 2. With a partner, compare your answers. Then practice asking and answering questions about the orders.

2 Pair Work

Step 1. Ask your partner questions about the schedule. Student A: Ask questions. Fill in the information that is needed.

Example: B: Did the notebooks arrive?   A: Yes, they arrived on June 15.

Delivery Schedule			
Item	Quantity	Arrived	Date
Coffee	2 cans		
Paper	2 cases		
Nails	2 boxes		
Screws	5 boxes		
Glue	1 case	✓	6/12
Ink	1 case	—	—
Notebooks	24	✓	6/15
Pencils	3 boxes	✓	6/15

Step 2. Now answer your partner's questions.

Student B: Ask questions. Fill in the information that is needed.

Example: A: Did the paper arrive?   B: Yes, it did. It arrived on June 16.

Delivery Schedule			
Item	Quantity	Arrived	Date
Coffee	2 cans	✓	6/16
Paper	2 cases	✓	6/15
Nails	2 boxes	–	–
Screws	5 boxes	✓	6/20
Glue	1 case		
Ink	1 case		
Notebooks	24		
Pencils	3 boxes		

Step 3.   Compare answers with your partner.

3 Group/Class Work

With a group, write the order of dates and times. Write *1* for the first in each group. Number the others.

A. Tuan dropped the file of inventory forms. Write the correct order of the dates.

_____ 12/96   _____ 3/97   _____ 9/96

_____ 6/96   _____ 3/96

B. Marie needs help putting the job orders in the correct order by time.

_____ 8:15 A.M.   _____ 10:45 A.M.   _____ 7:30 A.M.

_____ 9:30 A.M.   _____ 3:15 P.M.

4 Culture Work

Rob lost an important paper: the supply order for some supplies for his boss. He doesn't have a copy. What can he do? Look at the possibilities below. Add your own idea at the bottom. Rank the possibilities in order from 1 to 5, from better to worse.

_____ He can just forget about it. His supervisor probably won't remember.

_____ He can tell his supervisor and ask for another supply form.

_____ He can think of an excuse and blame a co-worker.

(“I gave the papers to Jerry. Ask him about it.”)

_____ He can try to remember the order and fill out another form.

_____ _____

PERFORMANCE REVIEWS

Openers

Look at the pictures. Point to people who are:

happy   unhappy   careful   careless

Where are they? What are they talking about? What is the difference in these two pictures?

1 Listen and Think

Listen to the conversation and circle the correct answers.

1. Who is the supervisor?   **a.** 1   **b.** 2   **c.** 3

2. How many pieces did Binh finish?   **a.** 24   **b.** 240   **c.** 2400

3. How many pieces did Tom finish?   **a.** 9   **b.** 29   **c.** 109

4. When will Carol come to see Tom again? **a.** tomorrow   **b.** next week   **c.** next year

5. What does Binh want to learn?   **a.** to be a   **b.** to fix   **c.** to be an
                                             supervisor   machines   assembler

2 Talk to a Partner

Step 1. Practice the conversations with a partner.

A: Binh, can I talk to you a minute?
B: Sure.
A: I think you're doing an excellent job.
    You're hardworking and careful.
B: Thank you. I really try to do a good job.

A: Tom, can I talk to you a minute?
C: Sure.
A: You didn't finish all the work.
C: Oh, I'm sorry.
A: You're not doing a good job.
    Please be more careful.
C: I'll try to do better.

Name	Work Record	Characteristics
Binh	excellent	hardworking
Tom	poor	lazy
Emma	good	careful
Olga	poor	careless

Step 2. With your partner, create similar conversations for the other workers.

3 Read and Think

Step 1. Look at the picture. Binh's company gave him an award for good work.

Step 2. Read the text.

Acme Metal Company would like to congratulate Binh Van Tran, the "Employee of the Month" for May 1997. Binh is in his third year as an assembler in the production department. He is a hardworking employee with excellent performance evaluations.

Supervisor Carol Baker says, "Binh does his work well and on schedule. He cares about his work, and he keeps his work area neat and organized. Binh gets along well with others and often has to train new employees in the procedures and routine. It's a pleasure to have Binh on our team."

Step 3. Look at the vocabulary on page 87. Then read the text again.

Vocabulary

Company Organization

routine the order and way things are done
evaluation a summary of how well things are going
schedule a plan that shows when, who, and where things are happening
supervisor a boss or person who oversees some workers
department one part of a company
award a prize
performance the quality of an employee's work

Skills

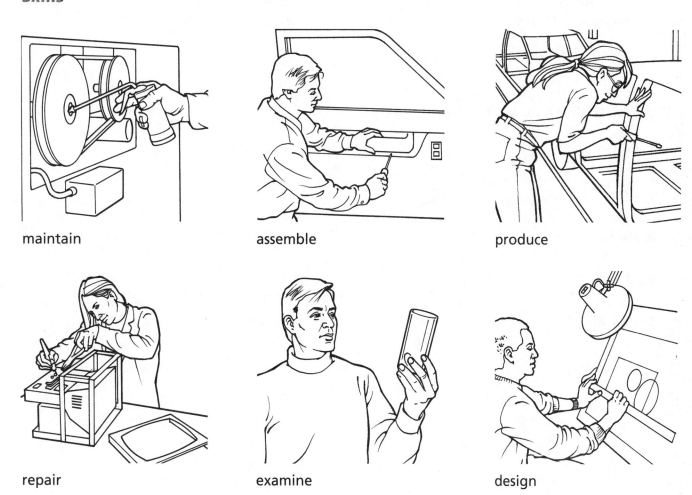

maintain

assemble

produce

repair

examine

design

Word Practice

A. Fill in the missing words.

departments	award	performance
supervisor		evaluation

1. Did the company give an _____ *award* _____ for the best worker?

2. The _____ can answer your questions about the job and explain what to do.

3. Every year, the company does an _____ of how well people are working.

4. There are three _____ in this company: production, maintenance, and administration.

5. If I work harder, my _____ will be better.

B. Listen. Match the person with the skills.

1. Ben   **a.** design

2. Hong   **b.** examine

3. Paula   **c.** produce

4. Marco   **d.** maintain

5. William   **e.** repair

4 Put It in Writing

Answer the questions about yourself.

1. What skills do you have?

_____

2. How do you feel about your work (or school work)?

_____

3. Are you hardworking or lazy?

_____

4. What are your good points?

_____

5. What are your weak points?

_____

6. Are you usually on time or late for work (or school)?

_____

7. What would you like to learn for work (or school)?

_____

5 Listen and Speak

Step 1.   Listen to the conversation.

> A: Your work is very good.
> B: Thank you.
> A: How do you feel about your work?
> B: I think I'm doing well. But I'd like
>   to learn more about the **paperwork**.
> A: You should talk to **Sally** in the **Personnel**
>   **Department**. Maybe she can help you.

Step 2.   Practice the conversation with a partner.

Step 3.   Change partners. Practice talking about learning more on the job.

6 Read and Write

Step 1.   Read the performance evaluation.

Employee Performance Evaluation

Name: *Rita Caramelo* Date: *5/26/97*
Job Title: *Bookkeeper* Department: *Administration*

− unsatisfactory   ✓ satisfactory   + excellent

Punctuality
- starts work on time   +
- calls in if sick   +

Work
- hardworking   ✓
- follows instructions   ✓
- keeps area neat   +
- follows safety rules   +
- does work on time   ✓

Working with Others
- helpful   ✓
- cooperative   ✓
- gets along with others   ✓
- accepts corrections   −

Supervisor: *Norman Pelletier*

Step 2.   Write the answers to the questions.

1. What is the name of the worker? *The worker's name is Rita Caramelo.*

2. What is her job? _____

3. Is she a good worker or a poor worker? _____

4. What are the lowest scores for? _____

5. What are the best scores for? _____

Step 3.   With a partner, compare your answers.

1 You should talk to Alice in the Personnel Department.

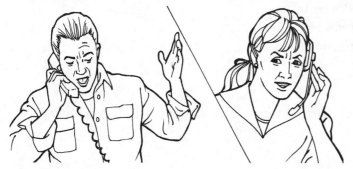

"I want my money back."

"You **should go** to the Customer Service Department."

Examples

She doesn't understand.
It's 3:00, but they finish work at 4:00.

She **should talk** to the boss.
They **shouldn't leave** early.

Practice 1

A. Listen. Circle the word you hear.

1. (should)   shouldn't   5. should   shouldn't
2. should   shouldn't   6. should   shouldn't
3. should   shouldn't   7. should   shouldn't
4. should   shouldn't   8. should   shouldn't

B. Match the situation to what you should do.

1. There's a fire in the workplace.   **a.** You should call a plumber.

2. There's no water.   **b.** You should call the machinist.

3. There's no electricity.   **c.** You should call 911.

4. Someone is hurt badly.   **d.** You should call in sick.

5. The machine is broken.   **e.** You should call the electric company.

6. You're sick and can't work.   **f.** You should call an ambulance.

C. Role-play. Give advice to a friend about the situations above. Change roles.

D. Where should you go to register for classes? get tax forms? find employment information? Tell a partner.

2 Binh is the best worker.

fast	(the) fast**est**
slow	(the) slow**est**
heavy	(the) heav**iest**
bad	(the) **worst**

Examples

The printing company is in a **large** building. The factory is **the largest** building in town.

Practice 2

A. Listen. Circle the word you hear.

1. cheap   (cheapest)

2. quick   quickest

3. neat   neatest

4. friendly   friendliest

5. good   best

6. pretty   prettiest

7. safe   safest

8. bad   worst

B. Fill in the correct form of the adjective.

1. This is the _____*best*_____ (good) evaluation of all.

2. Are you sure that this machine is _____ (safe)?

3. Hector worked there the _____ (long).

4. She's not a _____ (neat) worker.

5. Who is the _____ (friendly) person at work?

C. Work with a partner. Talk about people you know.

Who is . . .?
friendly?   the friendliest?
neat?   the neatest?
a good worker?   the best worker?

3 He has the same pay as our supervisor!

Pay to the order of	
Rhoda Helprin	Two hundred forty dollars
	_____

Pay to the order of	
Jane Wallers	Two hundred forty dollars
	_____

Rhoda gets $240/wk. Jane gets $240/wk.   Rhoda has **the same pay as** Jane.

Examples

He is 40 years old. Bill is 40 years old.   He is **the same age as** Bill.
Ben worked for 5 years. **Joan worked for 5 years.**   Ben has **the same work experience as** Joan.
Wendy is a hairstylist. I'm an assembler.   Wendy's job is**n't the same as** mine.

Practice 3

A. Listen. Circle = if they are the same. Circle ≠ if they are different.

1.	⊜	≠	**3.**	=	≠	**5.**	=	≠	**7.**	=	≠
2.	=	≠	**4.**	=	≠	**6.**	=	≠	**8.**	=	≠

B. Fill out the chart below for yourself. Then talk to two classmates. Ask questions to complete the chart.

	You	Student No. 1	Student No. 2
job			
nationality			
favorite sport			
favorite food			

C. What is the same? What is different? Tell the class.

4 I couldn't finish all the work. There wasn't enough time.

Present			Past		
I	**can**	finish the work.	I, you, he, she, it, we, they	**could**	finish the work.
	can't			**couldn't**	

Examples

I **couldn't find** a parking space near the company. I had to park far away.

I **couldn't tell** the difference.

My old job was very good. I had three weeks of vacation every year, and I **could take** it all at the same time.

A: They gave us a long speech in English the first day.

B: **Could** you **understand** it?

A: Yes, most of it.

Practice 4

A. Listen. Circle the words you hear.

1. could (couldn't)   3. could   couldn't   5. could   couldn't

2. could   couldn't   4. could   couldn't   6. could   couldn't

B. Complete the sentences with *could*, *couldn't*, *can*, or *can't*, as appropriate.

1. I (not call) _____ *couldn't call* _____ yesterday. There wasn't a phone anywhere.

2. Debby (not find) _____ a job until March. She was unemployed for a long time.

3. At his old job, Ralph (arrive) _____ at work anytime between 7:00 and 10:00.

4. Usually, they (find) _____ temporary workers very easily.

5. Lauren (not read) _____ the warnings. They were in Spanish.

C. Think about the differences between your native country and the U.S. What could you do there, and what couldn't you do? What can you do here, and what can't you do? Tell a partner.

Example: I'm from Moscow. In Moscow, I couldn't take the subway after 1:00 in the morning. The subway closed at 1:00. Here I can't take long vacations. But in Moscow, I could take four weeks of vacation every year.

Putting It to Work

1 Pair Work

Step 1. With a partner, listen to the conversation and fill out the performance evaluation.

Employee Performance Evaluation

Name: *Joan Richards*   Date: _____
Job Title: _____   Department: *Sales*

         – unsatisfactory   ✓ satisfactory   + excellent

Punctuality
- starts work on time
- calls in if sick

Work
- follows instructions   ✓
- follows safety rules
- does work on time
- accepts corrections

Working with Others
- helpful
- cooperative
- gets along with others

Supervisor: *Norman Pelletier*

Step 2. Talk to another pair of classmates. Compare your answers.

2 Pair Work

Step 1. With a partner, look at the picture on page 85. How would you evaluate Binh and Tom?

    – unsatisfactory   ✓ satisfactory   + excellent

Work	Work
• hardworking	• hardworking
• does work correctly	• does work correctly
• keeps area neat	• keeps area neat
• does work on time	• does work on time
Working with Others	**Working with Others**
• helpful	• helpful
• cooperative	• cooperative

Step 2. Role-play with your partner a conversation between the supervisor and the worker.

3 Group/Class Work

Self-evaluation: Fill out the form about your work or your classwork. Talk about your evaluation in groups.

Performance Evaluation

Name: _____   Date: _____

+ excellent   3 satisfactory   − unsatisfactory

Attendance
• always at work/class
• always on time

Work
• hardworking
• neat
• finishes on time
• asks questions when
  doesn't understand

• follows instructions
• follows safety rules

Working with Others
• helpful
• cooperative
• gets along with others

Good points: _____

Weak points: _____

Ways to improve: _____

---

4 Culture Work

Some gestures mean something is good. How do you show that something is good?

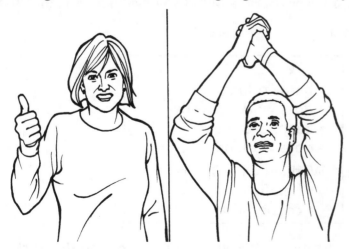

Unit 9
JOB PROMOTIONS

Openers

Look at the picture. Do the words below apply to the situation? How?

promotion   training   goals   career

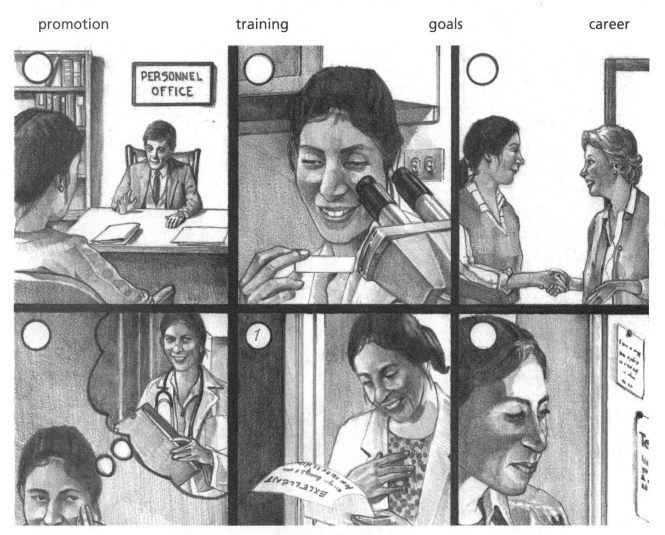

Where are they? What are they talking about?

1 Listen and Think

Listen to the conversation and number the boxes in the correct order.

2 Talk to a Partner

Step 1. Practice the conversation with a partner.

A: Elenora, I see your supervisor gave you a good review.
   She says you're an excellent **lab assistant**.
B: I'm glad to hear that.
A: You're **the most qualified lab assistant** here.
   In fact, you're too qualified.
   And we're looking for a new **lab technician**.
   Are you interested?
B: **Yes, I am, definitely**.
A: Well, then, you can start **next week**.
B: That's great! May I ask a question?
A: Sure, go ahead.
B: Does this mean a salary increase, too?
A: Yes, it does.

receptionist	....	secretary
chef's helper	...	chef
housekeeper	...	supervisor

Step 2. Change partners. Practice talking about other job promotions.

3 Read and Think

Step 1. Look at the picture. Sedar has a new job. His old job didn't pay enough.

Step 2. Read the text.

Sedar started at the hospital as a janitor. It was easy for Sedar to learn the routine and work. He was a dependable and hardworking employee. But the salary was only $5 an hour. Sedar couldn't pay all of his daily expenses. Also Sedar wanted to learn more about other jobs in the hospital. Sedar saw an opening for a lab assistant, and he applied. Sedar got the job because of his good job evaluation and because of his supervisor's recommendation. Sedar is quickly learning his new job. He hopes to get some more training. His goal is to become a nurse. Sedar plans to work and study hard to achieve his career goals.

Step 3. Below is part of the organization chart for the hospital. Find Sedar's position on the chart. Reread the text on page 98 if you need to. Then find the lab assistant positions.

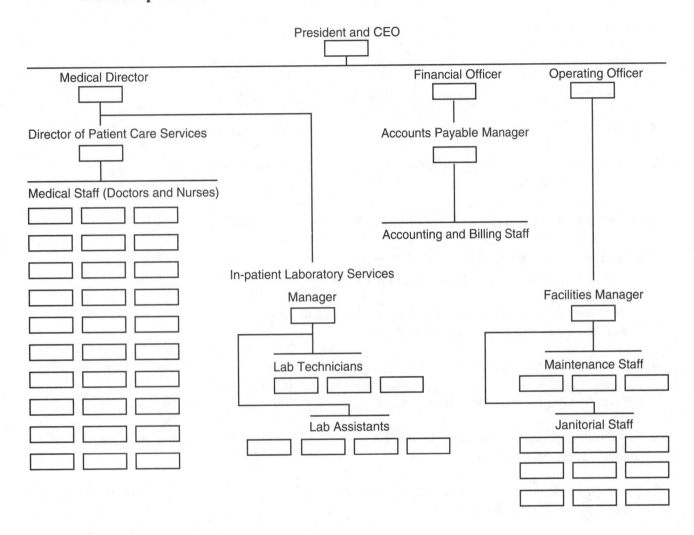

Vocabulary

Company Systems

promotion a change to a job with more responsibility and usually more pay

raise an increase in salary

career goals plans for future jobs

in-service training training you get while you are working at a job

course the name of a class

work history a list of past jobs

staff employees

recommendation a statement by someone that tells your good points

references people who know your work

maintenance keeping things in good physical condition

janitorial staff the entire staff of janitors

in-patient in the hospital (not outside)

facilities building and equipment of an organization

CEO Chief Executive Officer: usually, the president

Word Practice

A. Listen. Circle the correct word(s).

1. in-service training   (promotion)   raise

2. references   work history   career goals

3. courses   recommendations   promotion

4. raise   references   work history

5. career goals   courses   recommendations

B. Draw a line. Match the examples with the words.

1. janitor, Freetown Memorial Hospital, 2 years
   lab worker, Freetown Memorial Hospital, 1 year

2. Supervisor: Mr. Tucker, Freetown Memorial Hospital
   Teacher: Ms. Hopewell, Community College

3. I know Binh very well. He worked as a janitor.
   He was a hardworking, dependable member of the staff.
   He would be a good worker in any job.

4. Computer Accounting, Medical Terms, First Aid,
   English Composition

5. I want to be a radiology technician and later become
   a manager of the department.

a. courses

b. career goals

c. references

d. work history

e. recommendation

4 Put It in Writing

Answer these questions about yourself.

1. Do you have a job now? What is your job?

_____

2. What are your career goals?

_____

3. Do you need more experience or training for your goals?

_____

4. What training or courses do you need?

_____

5. Where can you take courses or get training?

_____

6. Who can you use as references?

_____

5 Listen and Speak

Step 1. Listen to the conversation.

> A: Hey, Al. Where are you going?
> B: To my **computer** class.
> A: You're studying **computers**? Where?
> B: At the community college.
> A: Why are you doing that?
> B: I want to be a **computer programmer**.
> A: Well, good luck with it.
> B: Thanks.

Step 2. Practice the conversation with a partner.

Step 3. Change the conversation. Substitute other classes and career goals.

Step 4. Talk about your own goals.

6 Read and Write

Step 1. Read the notices on the bulletin board.

Webster Health Clinic: Employee News.

1   Job Openings, May 12, 1997. Please ask in the Personnel Office if you are interested in any of the following job openings: Lab technician, Nurse: LPN, X-ray technician, Food server, Receptionist.

2   Annual Company Picnic. Join us for the tenth annual company picnic at Williamston State Park, May 27, 10 A.M.–4 P.M. Fun, games, food, surprises! Don't miss it! See Linda Harvey in Administration for more details. Be there!

3   Training Courses—Summer Session: EMT (Emergency Medical Techniques) training; Food, Nutrition, and Special Diets; Sensitivity Training; Aerobic Exercise; Dealing with On-the-Job Stress.

Step 2. Write the answers to the questions.

1. How many job openings are listed? _____

2. Are the salaries listed for the jobs? _____

3. Where do you apply for these jobs? _____

_____

4. Which jobs do not require a lot of medical training? _____

_____

5. What course would you take to be a cook in the hospital? _____

_____

6. Which courses might be useful in many different jobs? _____

_____

Step 3. With a partner, compare your answers.

1 The new position will be more interesting.

(1 syllable)		
fast	fast**er**	than
hard	hard**er**	
(2 syllables with *y*)		
speed y	speed**ier**	
(2 syllables)		
care ful	**more** careful	than
	less careful	
(3 syllables or more)		
dif fi cult	**more** difficult	
	less difficult	
hard work ing	**more** hardworking	
	less hardworking	

Examples

Jan works more than Ian. Jan is **more hardworking than** Ian. Ian is **less hardworking than** Jan.
Alice is **more careful than** Ted. Ted is **less careful than** Alice.
This job is **more difficult than** my old job. My old job was **less difficult**.

Practice 1

A. Listen. Circle True or False.

1. Carol works harder than Bob.   (T)   F   **3.** Jackie is more intelligent than John.   T   F

2. Jim is more careful than Sandra.   T   F   **4.** Randy is less interesting than Joe.   T   F

B. Complete the sentences below with the correct comparative forms.

This job is much (easy) _____ *easier* _____. The other job was a lot (difficult)

_____. My new job is (good) _____. Maybe I am

(hardworking) _____ than some people, or just (careful)

_____. My supervisor, naturally, is (experienced)

_____ than I am.

2 You're the most qualified person for the position.

qualified	**more** qualified **(the)**	**most qualified**
	less	**least**

Examples

May is **the most experienced**.

Lou is **the least intelligent** person here.

Of all my friends, she is **the most interesting**.

He's also **the least interesting**.

Practice 2

A. Listen. Circle the words you hear.

1. (the most)   the least

2. the most   the least

3. the most   more

4. the most   the least

5. the most   the least

6. the most   more

B. Complete the sentences with *the most* or *the least*.

1. Dale is (brilliant) _____*the most brilliant*_____ engineer in this company. He knows a lot about everything.

2. Gina has (fantastic) _____ job of all my friends. She's an architect.

3. Ralph is (interesting) _____ person at the company. He tells lots of great stories about Australia.

4. Ron is (competent) _____ programmer here. He never does anything right.

C. Talk to a partner. Think about the people in your class.

Who is the most intelligent? the most interesting? the most likeable?

Who is very intelligent? interesting? likeable?

Now give your partner a compliment. Say something nice to him or her.

3 May I ask a question?

May I **take** a break?

Can I **take** a break?

I need a break.

Use *may* with supervisors. Use *can* with co-workers and friends, or in informal situations.

Examples

May I **leave** early today?
Can we **finish** this tomorrow?

Sure, that will be fine.
Sorry, but no. It has to be done now.

Practice 3

A. Listen. Circle the word you hear. Circle – if you don't hear *may* or *can*.

1. may (can) –
2. may can –
3. may can –
4. may can –

5. may can –
6. may can –
7. may can –
8. may can –

B. In the sentences below, which is better? Complete the sentences with *may* or *can*.

1. (To a supervisor) Excuse me, _____*may*_____ I ask you a question?

2. (In a department store) _____ I help you?

3. (In class) _____ I help you with that?

4. (To a friend) _____ I call you back later? I have to do something.

5. (To a co-worker) I'm going to the cafeteria. _____ I get you something?

C. Look at each picture. Write a question asking permission.

1.

_____

_____

2.

_____

_____

3.

_____

_____

4.

_____

_____

D. Work with a partner. Role-play. Ask for permission in the situations below. Change roles.

Situation 1. You want to talk to your supervisor about a vacation. You want to take a vacation next month. Is that too soon? _Student A:_ You're the employee. First ask permission to talk to your supervisor. Then explain your situation. Finally, ask permission to take a vacation. _Student B:_ You're the supervisor.

> **Example:**   A: May I talk to you for a minute?
>   B: Sure, sit down.

Situation 2. You need to go home early. Your husband/wife is suddenly very ill. _Student A:_ You're the employee. First ask permission to talk to your supervisor. Then explain your situation. Finally, ask permission to go home right away (three hours early). _Student B:_ You're the supervisor.

Situation 3. You need to see a doctor, but the only appointments are during work hours. You want to ask your supervisor for two hours off next Thursday. _Student A:_ You're the employee. First ask permission to talk to your supervisor. Then explain your situation. Finally, ask permission to take two hours off next Thursday. _Student B:_ You're the supervisor.

Putting It to Work

1 Pair Work

Step 1. Listen and fill in the words in the correct places.

| nutrition | first aid | food server | lab assistant |
| chef | lab technician | food preparation | biology |

	Neil	Alicia
Present job	_____	_____
Promotion	_____	_____
Training wanted	_____	_____
Career goals	_____	_____

Step 2. With a partner, compare your answers.

Step 3. Ask and answer questions about the orders.

2 Pair Work

Step 1. Ask a partner questions about Fred and Maggie.

Student A: Ask questions about Fred. Fill in the information that is needed.

Example: A: What's Fred's job? B: He's a **gas station attendant**.

	Fred	Maggie
Present job	*gas station attendant*	store clerk
Job applied for	_____	cashier
Career goals	_____	bookkeeper
Training needed	_____	accounting, computer

Step 2. Now answer your partner's questions about Maggie.

Step 1.   Student B: Answer your partner's questions about Fred.

	Fred	Maggie
Present job	gas station attendant	*store clerk*
Job applied for	mechanic	
Career goals	manager of repair shop	
Training needed	business management, auto mechanics	

Step 2.   Now, ask questions about Maggie. Write down the information.

Example: B: What's Maggie's job? A: She's a **store clerk**.

Step 3.   Compare answers with your partner.

3 Group/Class Work

Interview three friends about their job plans. Write their answers in the chart.

Name			
Present Job			
Career Goals			
Training Needed			

4 Culture Work

Talk about training and education. With the class, discuss the questions below.

Where can adults go to school? What are the names of some schools and programs in your city or town? How much does it cost?

How is adult education in the U.S. the same as in your native country?
How is it different?

Unit 10
DOCTORS AND DENTISTS

Openers

Look at the picture. Point to these people and things:

doctor
eye test chart

scales
thermometer

blood pressure
x-ray

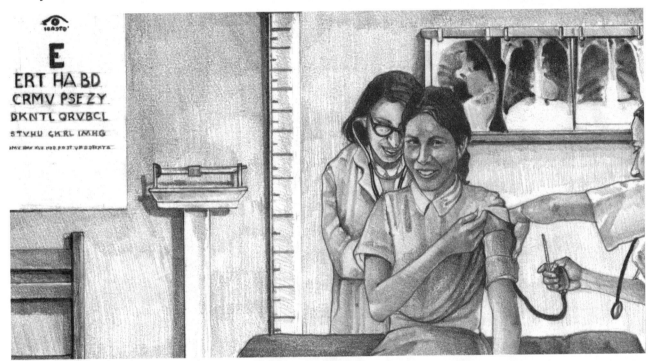

Where are they? What are they talking about? Why is Elenora there?

1 Listen and Think

Listen to the conversation. Then match the command with what the doctor is checking.

1. Step on the scales.

2. Read the first line of the eye chart.

3. Put the thermometer in your mouth.

4. Open your mouth.

5. Put this on your arm.

6. Take a deep breath.

a. Check your blood pressure.

b. Look at your throat.

c. Measure your weight and height.

d. Listen to your heart and lungs.

e. Test your eyes.

f. Check your temperature.

2 Talk to a Partner

Step 1. Practice the conversation with a partner.

A: Good afternoon. Doctor Crane's office.
B: Good afternoon. This is **Sokhom Sopal**.
   I need to make an appointment.
A: What's the problem?
B: **I have a cough and a fever.**
A: What's your temperature?
B: **102 degrees.**
A: Can you come today at **3:30**?
B: That will be fine.
A: OK. Doctor Crane will be able to see
   you then.

Step 2. Change partners. Practice calling for an
appointment for other problems.

3 Read and Think

Step 1. Look at the picture. Elenora is buying
medication at a pharmacy.

Step 2. Read the text.

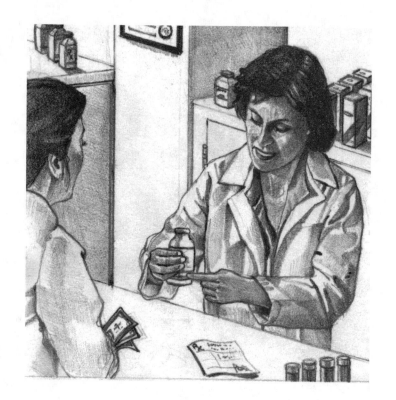

The doctor gave Elenora a
prescription for some medicine
for her cough. After the check-up
Elenora went to the pharmacy to
get the prescription filled. The
pharmacist explained the directions
to Elenora.

"Take one tablespoon every six
hours," he said. "Try to take it after
eating." He also explained that the
medicine might make Elenora
sleepy.

Elenora has health insurance
from her job. Most of the doctor's
bill and the medicine are covered or
paid for by the insurance company,
but Elenora still needs to pay a
small amount of the bills. She pays
$5 for each doctor's visit and $3 for
each prescription medicine.

Step 3. Read the label below. With some medications, it's bad to drink alcohol. What about the ones below? What should Elenora do? What shouldn't she do?

Elumyxtin
Take two tablets morning and evening, with or after a meal. Keep out of reach of children.

Toccitol
Take two tablets, twice a day. Warning: Do not take with alcohol. Do not drive or operate heavy machinery. Keep out of reach of children.

Helcitane
Take three capsules in the morning after breakfast. Warning: Do not take in the evening. Do not take on an empty stomach. Keep out of reach of children.

Vocabulary

Check-ups

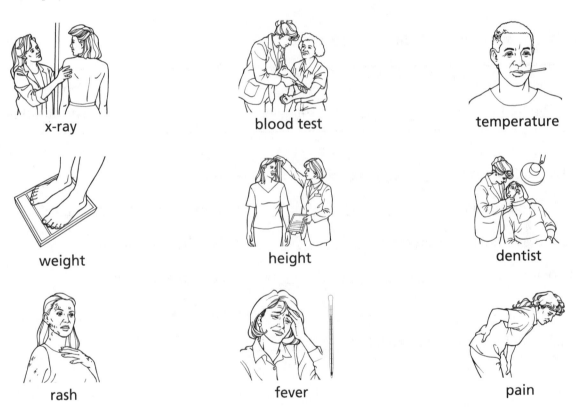

x-ray

blood test

temperature

weight

height

dentist

rash

fever

pain

Insurance

prescription   a written order from the doctor for special medicine

health insurance   something that helps pay for medical bills

dental insurance   something that helps pay for dental bills or bills related to a dentist's work on your teeth

policy   a written agreement with an insurance company

medical bill   the cost for a doctor and treatment

benefits   the money that the insurance company pays for the medical bill

Practice

A. Write the words in the correct categories.

temperature	doctor	nurse	policy
fever	pain	rash	x-ray
benefits	height	dentist	medical bill

people	reasons to see a doctor	insurance terms	check-up
doctor	_____	_____	_____
_____	_____	_____	_____
_____	_____	_____	_____

B. Fill in the missing words in the sentences.

height	pain	policy
temperature	dentist	prescription

1. John has a fever. His _____temperature_____ is 101 degrees.

2. Does your health insurance _____ pay for all of the medical bills?

3. I have an appointment with the _____ to check my teeth.

4. The doctor gave me a _____ for some cough medicine.

5. What's your _____? I'm five feet seven inches tall.

6. Hannah's tooth hurts. She has a lot of _____.

4 Put It in Writing

Fill out this medical history form about yourself.

```
┌─────────────────────────────────────────────────────────────────────┐
│                     Freetown Health Clinic                          │
│                                                                       │
│  Patient's Name _____        │
│  Address _____  Phone No. _____     │
│                 _____  Date of Birth _____    │
│  Employer _____    │
│  Do you have insurance? _____                                    │
│  Name of Insurance Co. _____  Policy No. _____     │
│  Date of last check-up _____      │
│  Did you ever stay in the hospital? _____     │
│  Are you taking any medicine now? _____     │
│                                                                       │
└─────────────────────────────────────────────────────────────────────┘
```

5 Listen and Speak

Step 1. Listen to the conversation.

A: I feel terrible!

B: Well, let me take a look. Hmm, I think you
have **the flu**.

A: What can I do for it?

B: I'll give you a prescription for some
medicine. Take **two capsules every six hours**.

A: **Two capsules every six hours?**

B: That's right. It should help your **cough
and fever**.

A: Can I go to work?

B: No. You should stay home for several days.

A: OK. Well, thank you.

Take 2 every 6 hours.

Take 2 before meals.

1 tablespoon at night.

Take 1 capsule every 4 hours.

Take two tablets as needed, not more than twice a day.

Step 2. Practice the conversation with a partner.

**Step 3. Change partners. Practice talking about other
problems and medicine.**

6 Read and Write

Step 1.   Read the prescription label.

Woodsville Pharmacy

6641589 02/19/97
DR. EDWARDS

JACKSON, PAUL

TAKE (1) TABLET
EVERY 6 HOURS AS
NEEDED FOR PAIN.

NO REFILLS

Caution: May cause
drowsiness. Alcohol may
intensify the effect. Use
care when operating a
car or dangerous
machinery.

Step 2.   Answer the questions.

1. Who should take the medicine? _Paul Jackson should._

2. What is this medicine for? _____

3. Who is the doctor? _____

4. How much of the medicine should he take? _____

5. How often does he take the medicine? _____

6. Are there any special instructions? _____

_____

Step 3.   With a partner, compare your answers.

Form and Function

1 I'll give you a prescription.

The doctor gave <u>me</u> **some medicine**.

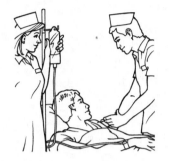

me	us
you	you
him	them
her	
it	

Examples

Brian told <u>us</u> **the problem**.
Who wrote <u>you</u> **that letter**?
The insurance company didn't send <u>me</u> **the information**.

Practice 1

A. Listen. Circle the word you hear.

1. me   you   (him)
2. her   them   us
3. you   us   me
4. them   her   him

5. you   it   us
6. him   them   me
7. you   her   me
8. us   it   them

B. Ask and answer questions with a partner.

Student A: Ask questions to find out what each person got. Fill in the type of medicine.

Example: What did the doctor give Mike?
The doctor gave <u>him</u> **some aspirin**.   •

Who	Type of Medicine
Mark	_____
Monica	capsules
Anton and you	_____
Betty	cold medicine
Tomas	_____
Kim and Li	eye drops

Student B: Ask questions to find out what each person got. Fill in the type of medicine.

Example: What did the doctor give Mike?
The doctor gave <u>him</u> **some aspirin**.

Who	Type of Medicine
Mark	tablets
Monica	_____
Anton and you	cough medicine
Betty	_____
Tomas	a prescription
Kim and Li	_____

C. Fill in the missing words.

1. Who gave Anton and you cough medicine? The doctor gave _____<u>*us*</u>_____ the medicine.

2. Who gave Tomas a prescription? Dr. Jones gave _____ a prescription.

3. What did Dr. Wong give Monica? She gave _____ a check-up.

4. Did Dr. Siva give Betty cold medicine? Yes, he gave _____ the medicine.

5. Did Dr. Siva give Tomas cough medicine? No, he gave _____ capsules.

2 He has different problems from the others.

John's leg hurts.   Julia's back hurts.
John has a **different** problem **from** Julia.
He has a **different** problem **from** <u>her</u>.
She has a **different** problem **from** <u>him</u>.

Examples

We have a **different** insurance company **from** the other workers.
He has a **different** supervisor **from** me.
Is your medicine the same as mine?   No, it's **different** medicine **from** yours.

Practice 2

A. Listen. Circle the word(s) you hear.

1. different   (different from)
2. different   different from
3. different   different from
4. different   different from

5. different   different from
6. different   different from
7. different   different from
8. different   different from

B. Look at the information about these people. Then fill in the missing words.

Name	Lana	Eduardo	Khamsao
Doctor	Dr. Siva	Dr. Connors	Dr. Connors
Ins. Co.	Blue Cross Insurance	Community Health Plan	Blue Cross Insurance
Problem	flu	flu	cough
Medicine	capsules	capsules	cough medicine

1. Lana has a different _____*doctor*_____ from Eduardo and Khamsao.

2. Eduardo has a different _____ from the others.

3. Khamsao has a different _____ and _____ from the others.

4. Eduardo takes different _____ from Khamsao.

5. Dr. Siva and Dr. Connors don't give different _____ for the flu.

C. Ask and answer questions with a partner.

> **Example:**   Who has different medicine from Eduardo?
> Does Lana have a different doctor from Khamsao?

3 Let's call the doctor.

> What should we do?   **Let's call** the doctor!

Examples

What do you want to do tonight?   **Let's go** to the movies!
Do you want to eat here?   No, **let's** not **eat** here.
Where do you want to go?   **Let's visit** Ben.

Practice 3

A. Listen. Circle the word you hear.

1. let   (let's)   **3.** let   let's   **5.** let   let's

2. let   let's   **4.** let   let's   **6.** let   let's

B. Write a suggestion for each situation.

1. Jonathan has a toothache.

Let's *call the dentist.*

2. We need to get a prescription filled.

_____

3. It's too cold in here.

_____

4. Isabel has a cold.

_____

5. I don't understand the instructions on this medicine label.

_____

6. Ben is in the hospital.

_____

Putting It to Work

1 Pair Work

Step 1. Listen to the conversations. With a partner, match the labels and the people. Fill in the missing information.

Novak, Pavel

TAKE _____

EVERY _____

CAUTION _____

_____

```
TAKE 1 TABLESPOON
EVERY 12 HOURS
CAUTION: SHAKE WELL
TAKE BEFORE MEALS

TAKE ONE TABLET
EVERY SIX HOURS
CAUTION: TAKE AFTER MEALS.
```

Lee, Kim B.

TAKE _____

_____ A DAY

CAUTION _____

_____

```
TAKE 2 CAPSULES
2 TIMES A DAY
CAUTION: DON'T TAKE FOR MORE
THAN ONE WEEK

TAKE TWO TABLESPOONS
THREE TIMES A DAY
CAUTION: DO NOT TAKE
WITH MILK.
```

Lopez, Annette

TAKE _____

EVERY _____

CAUTION _____

_____

Yates, Sergei

TAKE _____

_____ A DAY

CAUTION _____

_____

Step 2. Recheck the labels. Ask your partner questions about medicine labels.

Example: A: How much does Mark take?
B: He takes two tablets.
A: How often does he take the medicine?
B: He takes it every four hours.
A: Are there any special instructions?
B: Take it with milk.

Step 3. Role-play a conversation about one of the medications above. What should your partner do? What shouldn't your partner do?

Step 4. With another pair of classmates, compare your answers.

2 Group/Class Work

Step 1. What do you do for these problems? Explain your answers.

1.

_____

2.

_____

3.

_____

4.

_____

Step 2. Talk about the solutions with others in your group.

Step 3. Tell the class.

3 Culture Work

Who pays for doctor bills? Who pays for hospital bills? What happens if someone doesn't have insurance? Is this the same or different from your native country?

Jobs

a welder

a nurse

firefighters

a mechanic

a sales clerk

a janitor

a waiter

a carpenter

Tools, Equipment, and Parts

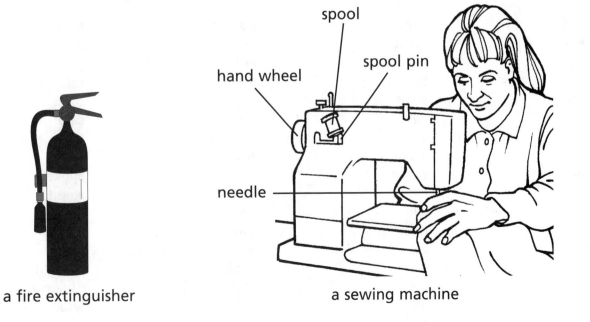

a fire extinguisher

spool

hand wheel

spool pin

needle

a sewing machine

clippers   a drill   a forklift   goggles

a paint roller   wire cutters   a welding helmet   a wheelbarrow

Appendix

Irregular Verbs

Present/Infinitive	Simple Past	Present/Infinitive	Simple Past
(be) am, is, are	was/were	know	knew
begin	began	leave	left
break	broke	make	made
bring	brought	put	put
buy	bought	read	read
come	came	ride	rode
cut	cut	say	said
do	did	see	saw
drink	drank	sit	sat
drive	drove	speak	spoke
eat	ate	stand	stood
feel	felt	take	took
find	found	teach	taught
get	got	tell	told
give	gave	think	thought
go	went	understand	understood
have	had	write	wrote
hear	heard		